VOICE-OVER
SUCCESS SECRETS

How to Make BIG MONEY
With Your Speaking Voice Without
Leaving Your Home

SUSAN BERKLEY

Campbell Hall Press

Voice-Over Success Secrets – How to Make Big Money With Your Speaking Voice Without Leaving Your Home

First edition 2020
Revised second edition 2021

Published by Campbell Hall Press, Englewood Cliffs, New Jersey.

This publication is designed to provide accurate and authoritative information in regard to the subject matter covered. It is sold with the understanding that the publisher is not engaged in rendering legal, accounting, or other professional services. If legal advice or other expert assistance is required, the services of a competent professional person should be sought.

Campbell Hall Press is a division of The Great Voice Company, Inc.

The Great Voice Company
1 DeWolf Rd Suite 205
Old Tappan, NJ 07675

We help men and women start and thrive in home-based businesses using their speaking voice. Are you interested in getting started in voice-over or growing an existing career?

Please visit www.greatvoice.com, call 201-541-8595 or email support@greatvoice.com.

To help you get maximum value
from this book, claim this collection of...

Free Voice-Over Resources
($97 value)
Waiting for you at:

www.GreatVoice.com/Gifts

✓ **FREE Audio Book:** *Voice-Over Secrets Exposed* read by Susan Berkley

✓ **FREE 6-Figure Voice-Over Success Roadmap:** video + workbook

✓ **FREE How to Get Started in Voice-Over:** 3-minute crash course

For the additional resources mentioned in this book, please visit:

www.GreatVoice.com/Gifts

TABLE OF CONTENTS

Part I

Part II

PART I

ONE

Make Money With Your Voice, No B.S.

Every day, thousands of men and women just like you are making great money with their voices from their home computers with nothing but an inexpensive microphone, some easy-to-use software, and an internet connection.

They're called voice-over artists, and they're recording everything from commercials to telephone announcements to web audio to fascinating audio books and more for clients all over the world.

Each year, thousands of companies set aside millions of dollars in talent fees to pay these voice-over artists.

Billions of dollars are spent every year on corporate audio and video productions that will never be heard on TV and radio, such as videos for websites, sales presentations, and e-learning programs. Voices are used for phone systems, audio books, and more.

The money-making opportunities for today's voice-over artist go way beyond commercials and corporate audio. I've identified 14 niche voice-over markets, some of which are enjoying explosive growth, and I'll explain each one in this book.

Some people think that celebrities get all the voice-over work, but actually that's not true. Sure, celebrities do commercials, and you might even recognize their voices.

But there are 11,341 commercial radio stations in the United States, with the average station running nine minutes of ads per hour. If you do the math, you'll see that's about 102,069 voice-over commercials every hour. A small handful of celebrities can't do all that work.

Most of the men and women who make money in voice-over are everyday people just like you. They do their work from their home studios all across the country.

And by the way, don't think you have to spend a fortune on recording equipment. You can set up a basic home studio for just a few hundred dollars. More about that coming up.

For some of these men and women, voice-over is a full-time career. For others, it's an enjoyable way to make some extra money on the side, a money hobby if you will.

The great news is, with the explosive growth of new media and the surge of internet advertising and technology, there's a huge and growing need for voice talent.

You probably have lots of questions about how to get started in voice-over as well as some questions about whether or not you have what it takes.

Well, I'm happy to help because the keys to voice-over success are probably not what you think. To be successful in voice-over, you don't need an exceptional voice, you don't need to invest a lot of money, and you don't need show business connections.

All it takes is understanding a few key secrets — and a great mentor who will guide and train you and help you follow the right road map to success.

Why I Wrote This Book

My name is Susan Berkley. If you don't recognize my name, you definitely know my voice. I'm the telephone voice of Citibank and AT&T. My voice is heard by millions of people every month. I still do voice-over every day, and I've made millions of dollars with my voice-over a long and successful career.

I've been featured in *The New York Times*, the *L.A. Times*, and on MSNBC, CNBC, and ABC News. I was also the behind-the-scenes voice and presentation skills coach for the winner on Donald Trump's *Apprentice*, Season 4. I guess you could say I'm a voice expert and voice-over super star.

But it wasn't always that way. Let me tell you who I used to be. I used to have a day job. But it wasn't just any day job.

My day job was being a radio DJ. Now you might think a job in radio is glamorous and high paying, but it's not. Sure, there are radio superstars, but the average radio disc jockey barely makes a living.

I started at a little radio station in Upstate New York and eventually moved to New York City to try to make it in The Big Apple. It wasn't easy. I had to work several day jobs just to make ends meet. I was a waitress, and I worked in a telemarketing boiler room selling deodorant crystals to funeral homes.

Then I got a job with a singing telegram company called Rent-a-Yenta. It seemed like it would be lots of fun until they sent me out onto 7th Avenue in New York City to deliver a singing telegram wearing a little elf costume. How humiliating.

To make matters even worse, it was a sweltering day in July. With my head hanging low and tears in my eyes, I trudged up 7th Avenue dressed like a Christmas elf in a red, fur-trimmed skirt with bells on my shoes thinking, "There has to be a better way."

Then I got my big break (or so I thought). I landed a spot as a traffic reporter on *The Howard Stern Show* and suddenly became famous. Now, you might think a show business job like this would pay big money, but it didn't.

While it was a lot of fun being on the show, I was still struggling to make ends meet, not to mention having to deal with being the butt of Howard's off-color jokes and bathroom humor day in and day out.

Now all this was right before *The Howard Stern Show* went into national syndication and Howard was about to become a household name. I could have stayed on the show and ridden his coat tails to fame and fortune.

But I had a dream to have my own business, my own voice-over business. And it wasn't going to happen if I was working as a low-paid employee in Howard's shadow.

I knew in my heart that I had to quit the show and move on, but the decision was agonizing. Maybe you've been at a crossroad like this in your life, too.

I felt like I was standing on a bridge looking down at a raging river. On one side of the river was the *Stern Show* with fame and potential fortune. On the other side of the river was my passion, my hopes, and my dreams. To get to the other side, I had to jump without a life preserver.

But that's exactly what I did. I held my breath, and I jumped.

I quit the show and nobody could believe it. It even made the papers! The listeners couldn't believe I was leaving, and Howard couldn't believe it, either. He called me up privately and asked me if I was crazy. I gulped and said maybe I was.

So, I thought about it and thought about it some more. And guess what I did? I asked Howard to put me back on the show. Have you ever regretted a decision and begged for a "do over"? That's what happened here.

I went back to the show, but I was more miserable than ever. And with every day that passed, I realized it wasn't for me. I worked up the courage to leave for good and start my own business.

And you know what? It worked. Within six months I was making more than my radio salary. And as the business grew, I opened my own production and training company, The Great Voice Company.

I'm happy to say that making the jump and starting my own business was the best decision I ever made.

Since 1987, The Great Voice Company has trained thousands of people in voice-over performance and business-building skills.

My production company provides recordings for hundreds of customers worldwide in all languages. I still continue to do voice-overs every day because I enjoy it so much.

I've come a long way from that struggling waitress in the elf costume. How did I do it? That's what this book is all about.

And you know what? I truly am glad to help. I am passionate about entrepreneurship and believe that America's small businesses are the backbone of our great nation.

I'm proud that I've helped create jobs and that my small business provides lasting value for our customers. And of course I'm proud of the great life I've created for myself.

But most important, it makes me happy to help you because someone shared his secrets with me when I was struggling and on my way up, when I really needed it most. And now, I want to pay it forward. Here's how it happened.

The Chance Meeting That Changed My Life

In the early days of my career, before I had a proven system for getting voice-over work, I'd sometimes get voice-over jobs by accident when someone heard me on the radio and liked my voice. But believe me, those times were very rare.

Then one day, I was doing one of those rare by-accident jobs with an actor named Bob.

Now Bob was a lot older than me, a real voice-over veteran, but he still sounded great.

As we finished recording and went out onto the street, I was fishing in my pocket for a subway token and he was getting into a beautiful Jaguar sedan.

Obviously he was getting a lot more work than I was. So I asked Bob (actually begged him) to let me take him to lunch, which was a big expense for me in those days. I really had to scrounge for the money.

I was hoping I could get him to tell me the secrets of his success. And you know what? He did. He told me that although he now enjoyed an amazing life because of his voice-over career, it wasn't always that way. He started out struggling, just like me.

But over the years, he had figured it all out in the school of hard knocks.

He not only had the beautiful car he always wanted, but he also had a beautiful home and lots of time to enjoy with his friends and family, especially his grandkids.

But what he was most grateful for was the ability to do something he really enjoyed because it felt like he never truly worked a day in his life.

Now he was getting ready to retire. With a catch in his voice, he said that before he left the business he felt like it was his duty to pass the torch and share his secrets with someone who would really appreciate them and put them to good use.

He smiled and said he thought that "someone" would be me.

Wow! I couldn't believe my good fortune.

We talked for what felt like hours. And Bob revealed many surprising secrets about how he grew his voice-over business.

Here's the #1 Secret to Voice-Over Success He Shared

Bob told me the most important secret of voice-over success is to find a good mentor.

A mentor is very important in voice-over work because you can't hear yourself as others hear you. It's an anatomical fact. You hear your voice inside your head where the sound is distorted by the bones of your skull.

Have you ever heard a recording of your voice where it sounds like a stranger? You think, "Is that really me?" Well, that's what I'm talking about.

To get really good at voice-over, you need an outside set of ears to coach you and show you the way. And you need a good mentor to show you the way to build your business, too.

Now, don't get me wrong. I'm not getting ready to retire like Bob was when he revealed his secrets to me. Not yet.

But I am getting ready to expand my business and take on some new projects, which means I'll only have time to work with a select group of voice-over newcomers who really appreciate what I have to offer.

Bob passed the torch to me. And now I want to pass it on to you, but only if you're someone who will appreciate Bob's wisdom.

Otherwise, it wouldn't be fair to Bob and it wouldn't be fair to me. I only want to work with people who will take action to make their dreams a reality.

If you are an honest, positive, action-oriented person, keep reading, because nothing makes me happier than to help you achieve success.

How to Know If Voice-Over Is for You

Can you see yourself in your comfortable home studio, no dress code required, doing interesting and creative projects that feel more like play than work, projects you can be proud of?

Would you enjoy an opportunity where no one is breathing down your neck — where you get to work when and where you choose?

Do you know or suspect you've been given the gift of a great voice, and do you want the recognition and satisfaction of sharing that gift?

Maybe you did some acting or radio in your early days, and those were the happiest days of your life.

Are you looking for an easy, part-time way to supplement your income working from home, a money hobby as I call it?

You can't deny that in today's economy everyone needs additional streams of income, some sort of gig on the side.

Do you have a spouse, friend, or loved one with a great voice you've always admired, and are you exploring this opportunity as a gift for them?

Are you imagining this would be the perfect way to spend your active retirement years?

After all, you certainly don't want to spend those precious years in a rocking chair.

Michael Turnbull wanted to avoid the rocking chair, too.

He sold a business he owned and was looking for an opportunity where he could make extra money using his voice but still enjoy fishing and playing golf.

At our voice-over Bootcamp Recording Studio Immersion Experience and in the private mentoring sessions that followed, I helped Michael develop his voice acting skills and position himself as the voice of the boomer generation.

He installed a small home studio and got to work. Now he's having a ball, voicing everything from commercials to narrations to announcements for events.

And he says the money's pretty nice, too.

But whether your goal is part-time income or an exciting new career, you might be feeling frustrated by the lack of to-the-point voice-over business-building guidance.

Or maybe you're looking for an experienced, caring mentor to take you by the hand and show you the way.

That's why you're reading this book right now.

A Remarkable Voice-Over Journey

I'd like to tell you a story about David Brower of Loveland, Colorado. David was the marketing manager for the eighth largest automotive group in the country.

He was planning to do voice-over when he retired, but he was still planning to work for a few more years.

Unfortunately, when the auto industry went belly up, so did David's job, and he was forced into retirement much sooner than he expected, but that's not all.

In the 100 days following the loss of his job, he had back surgery, was diagnosed with prostate cancer, and nine days later had a stroke.

Fortunately, David made a full recovery from both illnesses, but the experience gave him an acute awareness of his own mortality and caused him to look at things differently.

With his wife's support, David took a leap of faith and went full steam ahead into voice-over.

He attended my Voice-Over Bootcamp and several of our other programs so I could mentor him closely.

Working from home and recovering his health, he negotiated two annual contracts for voice-overwork that brought in about $3,000 a month, and he was just getting started!

Today, David continues to work as a freelance voice talent for the automotive industry and for companies including MetLife, HP, and the Gaylord chain of hotels.

David loves working from his home studio, especially the fact that he's just 16 feet from his coffee pot.

Plus, he has anytime access to the beautiful Harley motorcycle parked in his garage.

Whenever David and his wife feel like taking a little road trip, he just packs up his portable studio, puts it on the back of his bike, and hits the road.

He can record in the evenings from his hotel room.

During National Prostate Cancer Awareness Month, the Browers took a month off to ride 7,000 miles through 13 states to raise money and awareness for the disease.

David also travels at least once a year to Florida to see his son and his grandkids and always takes his portable studio with him.

He says he has so much fun it's a blessing, and he can't believe he gets paid to do it!

His advice for newcomers?

Believe in yourself and work hard, because no matter what anyone tells you, if you can find your niche and work hard, you will make money.

David also says to be sure you have a mentor and a coach.

66 I've been blessed to have Susan and her team in my backyard for many years. She's an invaluable resource for me, and I couldn't be as successful as I am without her."

Now, if you're thinking David Brower is one of the lucky few to reach this level of success, I would agree with you, but only to a point.

There is only one David Brower, that's true. But there are countless others who have achieved their own definition of personal and financial success in voice-over.

Let me introduce you to a few of them.

How Voice-Over Gave This Mom Her Life Back

Buffy O'Neill used to be a professional singer, but the late hours in smoky clubs kept her away from her two small children.

She loved singing but struggled with balancing her career and her family life.

Voice-Over seemed like the ideal solution. She started working part time at first, but gradually her career began to take off.

Now she says she has about 300 clients and works consistently for half of them, three or four times a week. The best thing about it is she can get out of the house for a few hours to run errands or spend time with her children.

Buffy's studio is compact, in a small addition to her home.

She and her husband made sure to locate the studio far away from the children's play-room so Buffy's voice-overs wouldn't pick up the sounds of the children playing.

For her, the flexibility of her voice-over business is one of the biggest perks. She can be a mom without feeling like she's away from the kids for 10 hours a day.

Buffy encourages newcomers to just go for it because, in her opinion, there's no better job out there. She says that even if she won the lottery, she would still keep doing her voice-over work.

Our students are teachers, IT profession-als, managers, engineers, bus drivers, doctors, and flight attendants. They are retirees and people getting ready to retire, moms returning to work, and even some very smart college stu-dents.

From Clueless Actor to Voice-Over Entrepreneur

When Dave Wallace came to our Voice-Over Bootcamp, he was in college to study acting. He says he has an artist's brain and until he met me had no clue what he was doing or how to run a business.

Now he says he gets a great deal of satis-faction from helping people grow their business by participating in their voice-over projects.

Since working with me, Dave has built an extensive client base. His customers like the sound of his voice, of course, but they also say he's a good business partner and very easy to work with.

Being customer focused was a revelation for Dave. As an actor, he was trained to think about how to portray copy convincingly or get into character. But once he started thinking about being more efficient and customer focused, he saw a dramatic increase in his income and client base.

Dave gets most of his jobs through networking, especially on LinkedIn. He also has business accounts on Twitter and Facebook and reaches out to potential clients who might be interested in his work.

He also makes sure he picks up the phone and calls people, which is something fewer and fewer people do these days. He credits me with giving him the scripts and the training he needed to do that.

To get leads, Dave looks online for production companies. Mandy.com is a great (and free) resource for that. But instead of approaching producers by email, he approaches them through Twitter, LinkedIn, and Facebook to give it a little bit more of a personal touch.

He asks if they are interested in somebody who specializes in the young, hip, cool sound because that's his niche. Then he sends them to his website to listen to his demos.

At the end of every communication, Dave says, "I look forward to helping you grow your business."

Just as he gets personal satisfaction from helping people to grow their business, he knows that, with every new project, his clients are also helping him. He approaches each job as a collaborative venture.

If prospects seem interested in him on social media, Dave sets up a call so he can talk with them in person and close the deal. His projects often lead to repeat business.

The good news is, for the most part he's supporting himself, and with each passing month, his business continues to grow. His parents are very happy about that.

His advice to newcomers? Tell your prospects you want to work with them rather than for them. Say you want to help their business grow and make life easy for them.

This type of collaborative approach makes you seem more human, and it really helps to bring in good business, income, and repeat clients.

Dave says:

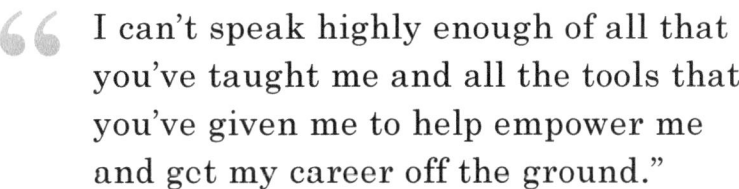

I can't speak highly enough of all that you've taught me and all the tools that you've given me to help empower me and get my career off the ground."

A Sudden Layoff and
Now a Silver Lining

Jay Webb used to work 50 to 60 hours a week for a local cable television company. His job kept him away from his young family where his wife was homeschooling their kids.

He yearned to quit the rat race so he could work from home and spend more time with his family. A voice-over business seemed like a good home-based business idea, but he wasn't really sure how to make it work.

Then one day, the company he was working for downsized and offered Jay a nice severance package. He talked to his wife, and they decided to go for it.

Jay tried to start his voice-over business on his own, but he just couldn't get it going. Then he discovered Greatvoice.com.

He attended our Voice-Over Bootcamp and quickly realized that voice-over was a business, not just "all show."

He started slowly, at his own pace, but then, by carefully following my marketing plan, it all started to come together, and he soon acquired new customers.

Jay has a warm, honest sound that voice buyers really love. Recently, we were casting a voice for a business audio book, and the client chose Jay. They really loved his voice.

In less than two years, Jay was able to earn a nice full-time income. I need to tell you that his results are not typical, and your results may be different, but for Jay and his family, it really made a difference.

Jay's home studio sounds great, but his investment was minimal.

He records in his bedroom in his walk-in closet, which is filled with clothes but still sounds great.

No one would ever suspect that he's recording in a closet and not in a professional studio.

The microphone he uses is a USB mic that plugs right into his computer. It sounds great and only cost $99.

He uses Audacity recording software, which is a free internet download. With the computer he already had, a closet, and 99 bucks, Jay was in business!

Jay's advice to newcomers?

> Make sure you get yourself trained. And don't forget, it's more of a business than you realize. Never forget the big picture. Without Susan's training, I would have been going into it completely blind. I didn't have any customers when I came to her Bootcamp, but after Bootcamp, I was set and ready to go."

As for the freedom and flexibility of his new voice-over lifestyle, Jay says:

I almost can't put it into words. I used to be tied to an office all day long. But now I can take care of the things I need to take care of, be with my family, and it's really beautiful."

TWO

How to Avoid the 9 Biggest Voice-Over Beginner Mistakes and Save Time, Money, and Embarrassment

Big Voice-Over Mistake #1:
They Use Auditioning Only

What's the worst way to start a voice-over career and make real money with your voice? It's trying to build your voice-over business solely by auditioning.

You'd be forgiven for making this mistake because everyone knows actors have to audition to get work. In fact, before the internet, auditions were the main way voice-over actors got work.

The internet has been a mixed blessing for voice actors.

The good news is it's opened up some extremely profitable technology-based streams of income for voice talent. The bad news is it's made it easier than ever to do more auditions, which can lead to frustration and broken dreams.

But before I tell you the good news about

how you can bypass auditions altogether as you grow your voice-over business, I want to make sure you fully understand why trying to auditionyour way to voice-over success is such a bad idea.

Prepare yourself for the real story.

A few years ago, several internet casting services known as "pay to play" hit the market. For a few hundred dollars a year, aspiring voice actors can pay to fill their in-box with auditions.

The idea took off, and now there are thousands of voice actors registered with these services.

But before you use the "too-much-competition" excuse to slam this book shut and run for the hills, I want to clarify a few things.

While some people book jobs using the pay-to-play services, they usually have to do many auditions to book a single job, sometimes hundreds of auditions.

The cold, hard truth is that many aspiring voice actors registered with these pay-to-play services never book a single job because they are poorly trained, not properly prepared, or because of too much competition for these auditions.

Their biggest mistake is following an audition-only business model, dreaming and hoping to get discovered but not doing anything practical besides auditioning to make that dream a reality.

When you join The Great Voice Company training programs, you won't have to concern yourself with the competition. You'll be playing an entirely different ball game where you are a category of one and the odds are stacked in your favor.

Voice buyers holding auditions can have hundreds of people to choose from if they wish.

However, in most cases, they don't take the time to listen to more than a handful of auditions, usually the ones that come in first. They zip through the auditions quickly, deleting most of them after a second or two, until they find a voice they like.

When you try to build your business through auditions, you can't nurture the relationship.

Often the auditions are blind and you don't have any idea who you are auditioning for. That's like asking a girl to marry you on the first date!

In business, you have to nurture your leads before they become customers.

Filling your pipeline with voice-over leads in your chosen niche markets and then nurturing them with time-tested marketing and sales techniques is the best and most reliable way to grow your business.

The selection process for auditions is subjective and out of your control. Often a voice is chosen on a whim or because of a feeling, with no real criteria at all.

I once landed a very big client because I was mistaken for another voice talent with a similar sounding name!

Fortunately they liked working with me a lot, and they are still my client decades later.

On the pay-to-play voice casting services (and with agents as well), you almost never get feedback on your auditions.

You don't know why you didn't get the job, so you can't work on ways to improve your performance. You might just keep on making the same mistakes over and over again and never be the wiser.

Now, don't get me wrong. I am not against auditioning. I still do it almost every day. I think the internet casting services are a good investment to build your skills and maybe even book something while you are at it.

But don't delude yourself. If you hope to get discovered in a voice-over audition and catapult yourself to fame and fortune, the best way to do it is to follow the proven marketing and business-building techniques I teach.

This is actually good news.

As I mentioned previously, very few people actually take the time to learn how to achieve lasting voice-over success, and that includes developing your voice acting skills, learning to properly record and edit your voice, and knowing how to position and market yourself as a category of one.

I'll dig into that in upcoming chapters

because it's the foundation of how great careers are built.

Big Voice-Over Mistake #2:
They Listen to Other Newcomers

Why is this so bad? Wannabes can give bad advice. Or worse yet, they can leave you discouraged and right back where you started.

I hate to say this, but there are even some people who will deliberately mislead you out of envy.

Some of these peers will indulge in bitch fests and spread negativity.

And for heaven's sake, don't play your demo for these people and ask them what they think.

Opinions are a dime a dozen. The only opinion that matters is that of the person who hands you a check!

Big Voice-Over Mistake #3:
They Ask a Local Broadcaster for Advice

There's a big difference between the announcing that DJs do as part of their radio jobs and the voice acting you do for big-ticket voice-over work.

I know because I use to be in radio.

To avoid spinning your wheels, you need to work with a voice-over specialist who can give you the right advice.

Big Voice-Over Mistake Number #4:
They Call a Talent Agency and Ask for Advice, But Then Get Doors Slammed in Their Face

This mistake is just plain naive. Some people assume that agents are sitting by the phone, waiting for newcomers to call.

But they're very busy people and get annoyed having to field calls from newbies.

Big Voice-Over Mistake # 5:
They Take an Adult Education Class at a Local Community College

These classes can be maddeningly superficial and are often taught by someone with little or outdated experience.

The result is incomplete information that gets you nowhere.

Big Voice-Over Mistake #6:
They Try to Take Shortcuts by Bypassing Training and Worse Yet, They Try to Produce Their Own Demos

These homemade demos are called kitchen table demos because they sound like someone stuck a boom box on their kitchen table and read some magazine ads into the microphone.

People send me these demos all the time. They're embarrassingly bad, and I feel so terrible for the poor people who send them.

I even heard there are some mean people in the industry who save these homemade demos and play them at the Christmas party for a laugh.

I don't want this to happen to you.

Big Voice-Over Mistake #7:
They Let a Friend in the Music Business Produce Their Demo

I met a woman who had spent thousands of dollars on a demo produced by a friend.

The demo had beautiful, custom-produced soundtracks, but the music overpowered the artist's voice and it sounded like she was drowning in a sea of strings.

Bottom line, her demo was useless.

Big Voice-Over Mistake #8:
They GRTGR (pronounced GRIT-grrr)

GRTGR is a term I invented that really resonates with my students. It stands for Getting Ready toGet Ready.

People with GRTGR are stuck.

They just can't get their career off the ground. They spend months trying to find the perfect web designer to create the perfect website and the perfect logo and the perfect color to go with their perfect brand. They feel paralyzed by their "head trash."

Fortunately, I'm an expert at helping people deal with their head trash to get them unstuck and back on track in no time!

Big Mistake Number #9:
They Give Up and Do Nothing

This is perhaps the worst mistake of all. Truth is, nothing will change unless you take the first steps and make it change. And that's what you're doing by reading this book.

So, congratulations! You're on your way!

Let's keep the ball rolling in Chapter 3 with my *Positive Performance Principles for Voice-Over Success.*

THREE

Positive Performance Principles for Voice-Over-Success

How to Find Your Money Voice — The Rashkoff Principle: Mrs. Rashkoff was my third-grade teacher. She taught me to love reading and about the beauty of the spoken word.

I'm really grateful to her because she instilled in me a love of words that became the foundation of my career.

Now, you may think voice-over is all about sound. But it's not. Voice-Over is actually a visual medium.

The big secret here is that people think in pictures, not words. When you read a voice-over script, your goal should be for the listener to see a movie in their mind as you speak.

That's what I call your money voice, and we're experts at helping people discover theirs.

When you are speaking with your money voice, your listener forms images in their mind and experiences feelings and emotions as you voice the script.

These emotions lead people to buy, and that means you become an in-demand voice actor who people will want to hire again and again.

The Big Difference Between Voice Acting and Announcing

A lot of folks think they know how to perform voice-over scripts because they took a class and someone taught them to stress certain words or bring their voice up or down at the end of sentences. But that's not voice acting; it's announcing.

Announcers are like dinosaurs — a thing of the past. Big money voice-over is not about putting on a phony radio voice. I call that announcer-itis, and it's a disease that can be fatal to your voice-over career.

Your money voice is not a phony voice, but an enhanced version of your natural voice. And that's you with focus, enthusiasm, and clarity.

Want to find your money voice?

The first step is a voice consultation with our Talent Advisor. Contact us at 800-333-8108 or support@greatvoice.com to schedule an appointment.

The Hot Potato Effect — Using Your Voice to Sell: The great sales coach Zig Ziglar said that selling is the transference of emotion.

To get someone to buy, you have to make them feel one of the trigger emotions, such as excitement, fear, or even lust. I'll explain.

Excitement is the trigger emotion we all feel when we hear about something new in an ad. We want to jump on the bandwagon so we don't miss out on all the fun.

The next trigger is fear. Many ads encourage us to buy out of fear of embarrassment, such as ads for deodorant or dandruff shampoo. Some ads, such as those for insurance companies, encourage us to buy out of the fear of loss.

And then there's lust. We're all adults here, so I won't mince words.

Sex sells everything from gadgets to clothing to cars to food.

Selling with your voice is transferring emotion from one person to another. The voice actor has to first feel the emotion, and then pass the emotional hot potato to the listener.

Top voice actors know how to put a wink in their voice, and they do this so effortlessly you are absolutely compelled to buy.

Relax! What Happens in Studio Stays in Studio: You've probably heard the saying "What happens in Vegas stays in Vegas," right?

But just as Las Vegas is the city that holds its secrets and will never kiss and tell, the recording studio holds its secrets, too.

The biggest secret is that the actors who record the voice-overs we hear every day made many mistakes during the recording process.

They don't read their scripts perfectly from beginning to end — far from it.

In fact, directors and audio engineers expect them to make mistakes.

But the listener will never hear those mistakes. All of the mistakes are edited out of the polished, final job. Even the sound of the actor's breath is diminished or removed.

It's just like kids playing basketball in a neighbor's driveway. Someone misses a shot and yells "do over." It's really no big deal.

Same thing in voice-over.

When the actor makes a mistake, he simply stops and reads the sentence again; later, he or the engineer edits out the mistake. No problem.

So, relax and take the pressure off.

Voice-Over is not like a theater play where everyone knows when someone flubs a line, or a live TV show where you can embarrass yourself in front of millions.

With today's easy-to-use recording software, you'll be amazed at how fast and easy it is to edit out mistakes, even if your tongue gets twisted and you make a really big goof.

Simply highlight the mistake and hit delete. Poof! Your mistake is gone, and no one will ever be the wiser.

The 3 A's for Voice-Over Success: The 3 A's are a key factor all successful voice actors have in common.

The 3 A's are: Always. Awesome. Accountability.

The most successful voice talents hold themselves fully accountable to their clients by actually doing what they say they'll do when they say they'll do it.

But they also hold themselves accountable to their coach.

A coach is vitally important to a successful career.

All actors and sports stars have them.

A coach provides a supportive environment where you can get expert guidance and someone to hold you accountable to fulfilling your voice-over career development goals.

Everyone can benefit from being held accountable by a coach, especially when you get stuck or run into obstacles you just can't overcome on your own.

Sometimes overcoming these obstacles requires you to step outside your comfort zone.

And you're a lot more likely to do that when you're being guided by an experienced and supportive coach.

To explore voice-over coaching options at The Great Voice Company, give us a call at 800-333-8108 or email support@greatvoice. com.

The Little Secret I Learned From Imus in the Morning That Made Me Rich: I'll never forget the early days of my career when I was a traffic reporter and cast member on *The Howard Stern Show.*

I was terrified. How was I ever going to stand up to Howard's teasing and his off-color jokes?

So, I racked my brain and asked myself who else in radio had a similar situation? How did they deal with it?

The answer was Charles McCord, former sidekick of the late radio talk show host Don Imus. Now, you might remember Imus from his *Imus in the Morning* nationally syndicated radio show and the shows he used to do on Fox TV.

Imus could get pretty offensive on the air. In fact, he had a long-standing rivalry with Howard Stern as to who could be more shocking.

But Imus's sidekick, the newscaster Charles McCord, never lost his cool. Here was someone I could model. Before I went on the air with Howard, I would think about Charles Mc-Cord and mentally download his cool, confident persona.

What happened was I inadvertently discovered a powerful acting secret: creating an avatar.

An avatar is an alter-ego character commonly used by players in interactive video games and virtual worlds online.

Externally, my avatar sounded and looked like me, but internally, she was completely different — tough and sassy, with the courage I needed to stand up to Howard on the air.

I've used this breakthrough avatar technique again and again in my voice acting career and teach it to my students.

These days I have another avatar called Phone Lady. I call on her whenever I record telephone voice prompts, such as those I do for Citibank. She's always on, always happy to take your call, even when I am not.

Phone Lady is an avatar, an enhanced version of me, and she's made me rich.

So, the big lesson here is, not all characters have funny voices. Often they sound exactly like you, but inside they're completely different.

This is the fun part of voice-over, where you really get to play.

A True Story About the Tremendous Money-Making Potential of Your Voice

An infomercial producer I know told me he had a very successful multimillion-dollar campaign for a kitchen gadget running on television.

If you've ever watched infomercials on

late night TV, you know what I am talking about.

One day, the voice talent he was using for those commercials called him and said he could no longer be the voice of the product.

He had a conflict with one of his other customers. But he did have a friend in the business who sounded just like him.

The producer was disappointed but listened to the friend's demo. Sure enough, he couldn't tell the difference.

To his ears, the two voices sounded exactly alike. So, the producer hired the friend and put his voice on the air.

Unfortunately, sales immediately began to plummet like a rock. The producer couldn't tell the difference between the two voices, but the customers could!

There was some-thing about the second voice that was unconsciously turning people off.

The panicked producer immediately called the original voice talent and offered him a lot of money to come back to the show and be their exclusive voice, an offer the talent couldn't refuse.

The producer put the original spot back on the air, and sales quickly climbed back to where they were before the switch.

The moral of the story?

Voice talent #1 had no idea how much his voice was worth, and you know what?

Neither do you!

Now, I'll bet you're wondering about your voice — do you have what it takes?

The answer is coming up next in Chapter 4, and it may surprise you.

FOUR

The Good News About What It Takes to Enjoy a Profitable Voice-Over Business

B y now, I'm sure you've realized that it takes more than just having a good voice to be successful in voice-over.

Your voice is important, of course, but there are some additional success factors to be aware of.

The good news is, you've probably mastered some of these success factors already.

I'll review them in this chapter.

Do You Have the Right Kind of Voice for Voice-Over?

Have you ever heard the expression "voice of god"? James Earl Jones has one.

In fact, the voice of god, or VOG, is a term casting directors use when seeking deep, rich male voices.

Many people think you need the voice of god to be a voice-over success, but that's simply not the case.

When I first started in voice-over, it's true that you had to sound like Richard Burton or a god. There were hardly any opportunities for women, people of color, or average-sounding people.

All that's changed today, of course. Voice buyers are looking for voice-over artists with a wide range of styles and voice types.

The voice of god is still used — which is good for guys with big, deep voices — but the market has opened up to all kinds of voices.

The #1 thing voice buyers are looking for? Anything but an announcer voice!

Today's voice actor is conversational and real, with a twist. You have to be able to read someone else's words believably, as if those words were your own.

So, the key to voice-over success is not necessarily the voice itself but the ability to sound like yourself reading someone else's words.

These days, voice-over is open to many different types of voices, and that's good news for newcomers.

How's Your Diction?

In voice-over, there is one obvious require-ment — people must be able to understand you when you speak.

If you mumble, you'll want to work on your diction so you don't swallow your words.

Following are some tips from my book *Speak to Influence, How to Unlock the Hidden Power of Your Voice*, available in bookstores and on Amazon.

Ready. Set. Warm Up Your Voice!

"Good speech takes muscle." That's what my voice coach, Mary Warren, used to say as she put me through hour after hour of exercises to strengthen my vocal articulator muscles to help me develop clear, clean, broadcast-quality speech.

Before I began working with Mary, I had no idea there were special exercises to improve these speech muscles.

But when I completed my voice training, I was so pleased with the results that I wondered why more people didn't do exercises to strengthen and improve the sound of their speaking voice.

The muscles that produce speech can become weak and flabby, just as the rest of our bodies do when they aren't exercised or used properly.

Just as it's important to stretch and warm up your body before a workout, it's also important to stretch and warm up the muscles you use for speech.

We take these muscles for granted.

But if you've ever lost your voice, you know how much you depend on it and how much you miss it when it's gone.

If your voice tires easily, sounds weak, or doesn't have a clear, resonant sound — or even if you have a good voice and you'd like to make it even better — please read on.

The exercises you are about to learn will help you:

- Develop the kind of voice people enjoy hearing
- Speak for hours without strain or stress
- Relax during important presentations, knowing you can count on your voice
- Improve the health of your voice
- Prevent problems, such as hoarseness, that develop with misuse
- Improve the clarity of your speech and diction
- Maintain a strong, healthy speaking voice at any age

If you are experiencing hoarseness, vocal weakness, laryngitis, pain while speaking, or any other throat or voice problem, please consult your doctor before beginning this vocal exercise program.

The vocal warm-up you are about to learn is safe and effective.

It was developed by Susan Miller, Ph.D., a certified speech language pathologist and scientific fellow for the American Academy of Otolaryngology.

She specializes in refinement of the speaking voice and treatment of people whose voices have been injured.

Dr. Miller uses these exercises to help her clients strengthen and rehabilitate their speaking voices. She has taught this warm-up program to broadcasters, politicians, professional speakers, and to people just like you.

It's helpful to sip water before and during these exercises.

And, now, let's get started!

Lip Flutters

This series of five lip flutters will help strengthen your vocal folds by providing resistance.

Although your lips will tingle, this is a warm-up for your voice, not your lips.

If you can't get your lips to flutter, place your index fingers on both sides of your mouth and press lightly.

Don't pucker. Make sure your lips are relaxed. The flutter is driven by your lungs, not your lips.

The goal is to vibrate your lips with the least amount of effort.

You can also get the same resistance effect by sticking out your tongue and making a "raspberry" sound or by trilling an "r."

1. **Lip flutters without sound**
   Close your lips and blow until you run out of air. Repeat three times.

2. **Lip spurts without sound**
   Make a series of quick, staccato lip flutters. See how many spurts you can do on a single breath.

3. **Lip flutters with sound**
   Close your lips and blow while making a steady tone. Sustain the sound as long as you can. Repeat three times.

4. **Lip flutters with ascending and descending scale**
   Flutter your lips while making a sound from your lowest note to your highest note.

5. **Lip flutter your favorite song**
   Flutter your lips to the tune of your favorite song. This is a challenging exercise that really develops breath control. While it may take some practice, it doesn't have to be perfect to achieve the desired effect.

The Siren

This exercise improves pitch range and vocal muscle tone. It's great for flat or monotone voices.

It stretches your vocal folds to keep them flexible and healthy.

While saying "who," glide a siren sound from your lowest note to your highest note. Keep your voice soft and nasal. Try to perform the glide smoothly without any breaks.

Keep your voice forward and out of the back of your throat. Don't raise your shoulders.

It's OK if your voice "squeaks." Eventually you will be able to do this exercise without any breaks as you glide from your lowest to your highest pitch.

Vocal Focus

This exercise helps you locate your facial mask and find your optimal speaking pitch.

Picture an inverted triangle, or mask-like shape, that stretches from your two sinuses to your larynx.

When you speak from the mask, your voice is amplified by the resonating chambers in your face, mouth, and throat.

Your voice sounds strong and resonant, and you are able to speak without strain.

To locate your facial mask, say "mmm" until you feel your lips vibrate. Don't be shy or soft. Give it a good strong, loud "mmm" until you feel your lips and nose tingle.

Now, let's combine humming and speaking.

Count from one to ten blending humming

into each number as you speak.

Say mmmone, mmmtwo, mmmthree, and so on. Try to blend the hum and the number into one continuous sound.

Sustain a Pitch

For this exercise you will need a pitch pipe, a piano, or other instrument to get the proper pitch for each tone.

You can buy a pitch pipe at a music store or online.

Do this exercise while standing. Softly sing the vowel sound "o" at C, D, E, F, and G on the musical scale.

Women should try to match tones from middle C to high C and men from low C to middle C.

Keep the sound light and soft. Do not push or strain to reach the high notes.

If the high notes are difficult to sing, begin your scale at B or even A below C.

A Vocal Health Tip
From Dr. Susan Miller

To determine if you suffer from a voice problem that should be diagnosed and treated by a doctor, make a hissing "s" sound like air escaping from a balloon.

See how long you can sustain the sound without running out of air. A speaker with a healthy voice should be able to sustain a hissing "s" for at least 15 or 20 seconds.

Next, repeat the exercise while sustaining a buzzing "z" sound for as long as you can.

If you are unable to sustain either sound for at least 15 seconds after repeated attempts, please see your doctor to determine if something — such as a vocal nodule or callous — is impeding the vibration of your vocal folds.

Maintaining the health of your voice with these exercises is simple and easy.

Do them at the start of each day and you should notice results within a few short weeks.

On days when you are pressed for time, omit the pitch-sustaining exercises and you should be able to do the lip flutters, siren, and vocal focus exercises in five minutes or less.

It's a smart investment of time for really big results.

Improve the Clarity of Your Speech

Do people tell you that you mumble? When you speak, do they often ask you to repeat yourself?

If so, it could be because your diction needs a little help. *The American Heritage Dictionary* defines diction as "the degree of clarity and distinctness in speech."

Vowels add color and consonants add clarity to our speech. But if you don't pronounce them properly, your speech will sound bland and indistinct.

The sentences below have been specially designed to work many of the vowel and consonant sounds in the English language.

They are not tongue twisters. Say them aloud slowly and practice them often to improve the clarity of your speech.

If you are unsure about the proper pronunciation of these or any other words, look them up and hear them spoken at the Merriam Webster dictionary website at www.m-w.com.

It's free of charge!

To improve your diction, speak these sentences slowly and clearly:

- *Green tea ice cream is a treat to eat.*
- *Amy aimed at the gate.*
- *Ed said, "Get into bed."*
- *This itchy sweater comes from Italy.*
- *Old folks row slowly.*
- *Tom was rather calm as he took the bomb from the box.*
- *Go with the flow to stay in the know.*
- *Juice makes the sauce more succulent.*
- *Buffy's tough buddy had fallen in love.*
- *The redhead fell at the sound of the bell.*
- *Take a whiff of these cookies before you eat them with your friends.*
- *Ask her if she wants to take on the task.*
- *Mean men may cause harm.*

- *Pay the mime a dime.*
- *His performance is sublime.*
- *She lost her poise after hearing the noise.*
- *Put the oily oysters on the doily.*
- *Sheila gave Dave a shampoo and a shave.*
- *I knew the crew in the blue canoe.*
- *It's our duty to salute the new recruit.*
- *The breeze made her sneeze as she walked through the trees.*
- *There was a shortage of blood because of the flood.*
- *Tell the truth to the rude recruit.*
- *Veronica put the vivid violets in the Victorian vase.*
- *The odd opera singer had a four-octave range.*
- *Todd placed the pot on the rock.*
- *The anchor signed off on the nightly news.*
- *Dirty deeds done dirt cheap.*
- *Throughout the night he thought things through.*
- *Emily's enterprise enjoyed success.*

Take the Tongue Twister Challenge

If you crave tongue twisters, I've collected a few of the classics for you below.

Try to say them as quickly as possible — and without mistakes.

- *A proper copper coffee pot.*
- *Around the rugged rocks the ragged rascals ran.*
- *Long-legged ladies last longer.*
- *Mixed biscuits, mixed biscuits.*
- *A box of biscuits, a box of mixed biscuits and a biscuit mixer!*
- *Peter Piper picked a peck of pickled peppers. Did Peter Piper pick a peck of pickled peppers? If Peter Piper picked a peck of pickled peppers, Where's the peck of pickled peppers Peter Piper picked?*
- *Pink lorry, yellow lorry.*
- *Red leather, yellow leather, red leather, yellow leather.*
- *She sells sea-shells on the seashore.*
- *Swan swam over the pond, Swim, swan, swim! Swan swam back again — Well swum, swan!*
- *Three grey geese in green fields grazing.*
- *We surely shall see the sun shine soon.*

And finally, the mother of all tongue twisters. This sentence has been described as the hardest tongue twister in the English language.

Say it if you dare!

- *The sixth sick sheik's sixth sheep is sick.*

All of the above exercises will help to improve the clarity of your speech, but there are several other aspects of what it takes to enjoy a profitable voice-over business.

So, let me ask you a few questions:

Are You a Fluid Reader?

While the ability to read copy smoothly is important in voice-over, the good news is it is not a live performance, so you don't have to worry about reading the script perfectly without making mistakes.

In voice-over nobody reads a script without flubbing lines, even the most experienced pros.

Mistakes are expected and can be easily edited out. Because most of the time you will be working from home, no one will ever know where you flubbed.

You'll just edit out the mistakes and send the clean audio recording to your customer.

Some people are naturally fluid readers. Others aren't.

If you are not a fluid reader, you'll save time if you improve your reading skills.

Sometimes improving your reading is as simple as a trip to the eye doctor to check your prescription.

Can you clearly see the script? Do you need new glasses?

Whether you're a fluid reader or not, your reading skills will quickly improve with practice.

A great way to get that practice while helping others is to volunteer to read for the blind or visually impaired.

Another way to improve your reading skills is to read the paper or a few pages of a book out loud every day.

Record yourself on your computer or smartphone and track how many times you break down or make mistakes.

Practice a little bit every day and you'll find that your reading skills quickly improve.

Have You Ever Acted in a Play?

Not everyone is a born actor. I'm certainly not.

In fact, the only play I ever acted in was *"You're a Good Man, Charlie Brown"* at summer camp when I was about 12 years old.

Hardly a memorable performance!

That was the last time I was ever in a play on stage, and I've done thousands of high-paying professional voice-over jobs since them.

The acting we do in voice-over is based on some of the key principles stage actors use with a few easy-to-learn distinctions.

The good news is, unlike stage acting, you don't need makeup, costumes, or time-consuming rehearsals.

My Perfect Performance™ method makes voice acting simple and gives you a series of easy-to-follow steps so you'll have the conversational sound voice buyers are looking for.

For more information on our voice acting coaching programs, contact us at 800-333-8108, support@greatvoice.com, or www.greatvoice.com.

The Three Components of Good Voice Acting

There are three components of good voice acting: relaxation, concentration, and imagination.

- ◆ *Relaxation* means you sound relaxed and at ease behind the mic. If performing on mic is a new experience, you might feel a little tense until you get used to it. I often suggest my students take a yoga class or practice relaxation exercises so they can call on these techniques whenever they need them to get focused and calm on mic.

- ◆ *Concentration* means you are able to focus on the copy to the exclusion of everything else that's happening around you. But it also means you are able to ignore and tune out any negative self-talk that's going on in your head while you perform. In my coaching programs, I strongly emphasize the voice-over success mindset, and I help my students overcome what they often call distracting "head trash."

◆ *Imagination* means you are able to conjure up a vivid image in your mind's eye as you perform your voice-overs. I've observed that in order for the audience to get a clear image of what the script writer is trying to convey, you, the voice actor, must see and feel it first.

Are you a people person?

Here's a key point I've observed while training thousands of people.

In voice-over, success has much more to do with getting people to know, like, and trust you, rather than with the sound of your voice.

I hope this brings you some relief because having a pleasing personality is something you can control. It's not subjective.

The good news is, if you've had any kind of work experience at all, you're probably already pretty good at getting along with others.

Any networking skills you've developed will translate beautifully in your new voice-over business.

Your Voice as a Marketable, Money-Making Asset

People sometimes ask me if I insure my voice. That makes me smile.

After all, my voice is a valuable money-making asset, and I'm sure Lloyd's of London would write me a policy… for a price.

The answer is no, I haven't insured my voice. But I have "insured" that I know as much as I can about selling and marketing my voice and my studio.

It's the smart way to take advantage of the astounding voice-over opportunity.

Our students at The Great Voice Company love our programs because of this marketing and sales oriented approach.

While we teach you the fun and enjoyable performance skills and the easy home studio skills you need to know, we want to make sure you know how to monetize your voice.

I'll be telling you exactly how to do that in an upcoming section about opportunity in the 14 Voice-Over Niche Markets.

But before I do, there's more to say about the "voice" in voice-over. After all, you can't have a successful career in voice-over unless you keep your voice in tiptop shape.

So, the next two chapters focus on the physical health of your voice and how mental and emotional factors such as stress and fear can affect speaking.

FIVE

How to Keep From Losing Your Voice (Even When Everyone Around You is Sneezing and Coughing in Your Face)

I f you've ever been concerned about the health of your voice, the information in this chapter is for you.

To get the lowdown on proper voice care, some years ago I interviewed Dr. Wallace Rubin, a top Ear, Nose, and Throat doctor.

Before his death in 2017, Dr. Rubin was a clinical professor of Otorhinolaryngology and Biocommunication at Louisiana State University School of Medicine.

He also had a private practice in New Orleans where he treated professional opera singers and other performers.

Here's what I learned from Dr. Rubin:

The Causes of Laryngitis

Laryngitis results from a swelling of the mucus membrane over the vocal chords. It is usually caused by a bacterial or viral infection or by an allergy affecting the respiratory tree.

The respiratory tree has a mucus lining that Dr. Rubin compared to a wall-to-wall carpet running through a house.

The lining begins at the nose and sinuses and continues past the voice box into the lungs. This lining contains protective chemicals that usually prevent infections in the nose, sinus, or lungs from spreading to other parts of the respiratory tree.

But sometimes the protective chemicals don't work, and an infection in the lungs or nose attacks the voice box.

In the wintertime, the warm, heated air we breathe dries out the mucus membranes and the protective chemicals along the respiratory tract, making us more vulnerable to infection.

Therefore, we are more likely to develop laryngitis during the winter months when infections are more prevalent and heaters are turned on.

How to Lessen Your Chances of Losing Your Voice

According to Dr. Rubin, the best thing to do is to humidify your environment, especially while you sleep. Do this by turning down the heat at night and running a humidifier.

But be careful about the kind of humidifier you use.

Cool mist humidifiers can promote the

growth of molds and yeast, causing allergies. Warm mist humidifiers are less likely to do so.

Some humidifiers add ultraviolet light for further sterilization. No matter which kind of humidifier you use, be sure to clean it frequently, following the manufacturer's directions.

Air purifiers are also helpful in removing allergens from your environment.

If you work in a crowded office, you'll be happy to know that it's difficult to catch a sore throat by using someone else's telephone.

Dr. Rubin told me that sore throat germs are usually transmitted by airborne particles in coughs or sneezes. You can also get sick by sharing infected silverware or glasses.

Washing your dishes in the dishwasher will sterilize them.

Sore Throat Rx

If you get a sore throat and your symptoms are mild, Dr. Rubin told me you can safely wait a day or two before seeing the doctor.

Things should improve if you get extra rest, eat well, and increase your fluid intake. If you are feeling at all under the weather, skip your regular workout session.

Vigorous exercise can temporarily lower your immunity and make things worse.

Dr. Rubin also advised against drinking alcohol while sick because of its dehydrating effects. See your doctor right away if your sore throat is accompanied by a fever or if your symptoms persist or worsen after 48 hours.

According to Dr. Rubin, too many doctors prescribe antibiotics over the phone without conducting the tests necessary for a proper diagnosis.

The symptoms of viral and bacterial infections are often the same. In fact, what you think is a cold can actually be an allergy with a secondary infection.

Once a simple blood count or smear of the nasal secretions is done, the doctor can tell immediately if the problem is bacterial, viral, or allergic and prescribe the proper treatment for your problem.

Only bacterial infections respond to antibiotics. Antibiotics can cause side effects, so take them only if you really need them.

If your throat problems are caused by a virus, prescription medications are now available that will help build your immunity.

Once the infection is addressed, your doctor may prescribe additional medications for swelling and blockage such as antihistamines, decongestants, and nasal steroids.

With proper treatment, many people can recover their voice in as little as 24 hours.

The next time you get a cold or allergy attack, think twice before reaching for an over-the-counter nasal spray.

Dr. Rubin said those over-the-counter nasal sprays, which affect the autonomic nervous system, such as Neo-Synephrine or Afrin, should be used only as directed on a short-term basis.

These sprays open clogged nasal passages by causing immediate shrinking of the mucous membranes; however, as the medication wears off, the membranes swell again.

The more you use these sprays, the less the membranes shrink and the more they swell.

Over time, more and more of the medication will be needed to achieve the desired effect.

How to Ensure the Health of Your Voice

Break the Throat Clearing Habit: Sore throats, whether caused by allergies or infection, are often accompanied by postnasal drainage dripping on the vocal cords.

When this happens, the urge to clear the throat is instinctual.

If the situation is chronic, throat clearing can become habitual, irritating the vocal cords.

According to Dr. Rubin, clearing a sore, irritated throat is like banging a swollen arm or leg against the wall.

He encouraged his patients to try and

swallow instead. It can be difficult to change your habit pattern because it's a lot more pleasing to clear your throat than it is to swallow, but if you can avoid the clearing reflex, you'll get well faster.

Drink Lots of Water: At least eight glasses a day is best. You may want to drink even more in the winter to counteract the drying effects of central heating.

Fluids like unsweetened fresh fruit juices are also helpful, but too much coffee or tea can be dehydrating.

Stay Away from Cigarettes: Cigarette smoke is so irritating that even nonsmokers will become hoarse after a night in a smoky bar.

Go Easy on Your Voice: Prolonged screaming or yelling to an audience can stress the vocal cords and cause swelling.

When speaking in public, use a microphone whenever possible.

Allergies and the Voice

If you suffer from hay fever and are sensitive to trees, grass, and pollen, you know it.

But many people don't know that food sensitivities can also cause allergic symptoms and problems with the voice.

If you are allergic to something you inhale, you will probably know it almost immediately.

But food allergies can take as long as 72 hours to appear, so you may need to see an allergist for diagnosis and treatment.

To determine if you suffer from a food allergy, your doctor may conduct a "provocative" food or chemical test.

Certain suspicious foods are eliminated from the diet and then reintroduced one by one to see what happens.

First, you avoid the suspected food or chemical for a number of days.

Then, you expose yourself following your doctor's instructions on the day prior to your office visit.

The most common food allergens are milk, dairy, soy, wheat, peanut, and egg. Dr. Rubin told me there is no need to suffer from allergies.

Your doctor can prescribe medication to take after you've been exposed to an allergen to prevent attacks from occurring.

Allergies and illness aren't the only things that can wreak havoc on your voice.

So can nerves.

In the next chapter, I share the ways you can manage your nerves and become a stress-free voice-over artist.

SIX

How to Be a Stress-Free Voice-Over Artist

Did you know that the fear of public speaking is the number one fear? Worse even than the fear of death? Yet just about everyone has experienced some degree of speech fright at some time in their life, even those whose speaking skills we admire.

Actors, athletes, and public figures know all about the delicate balance between anxiety and energy.

Sir Laurence Olivier, Helen Hayes, Luciano Pavarotti, Carly Simon and Barbra Streisand all admitted they suffered from nervousness and stage fright.

Speech fright can strike in front of an audience of any size, even over the phone.

It can even strike when you are recording a voice-over, even if you're the only one in the room.

The act of recording your voice can give rise to the same fear of public speaking. After all, the "speech" you are making will one day be made public!

Plus, there may be times when you are directed by someone else in the room or when a client wants to observe you in action.

The same tips that help someone who is giving a live speech will help you when you record your voice.

That is why I use the terms stage fright and speech fright interchangeably.

What Causes Speech Fright?

To begin with, it is important to understand that the symptoms of speech fright — the pounding heart, sweaty palms, trembling voice, and anxious feelings — are a perfectly normal reaction to acute stress.

These unpleasant, scary, and even debilitating symptoms are actually the effects of a stress-induced adrenaline rush.

There are several proven techniques that can be used to burn off the excess adrenaline before a presentation or recording session to make speaking a more comfortable experience.

I'll share these methods a little later in this chapter.

A few exercises may be all you need if your speech fright is mild.

But if your fear of public speaking is affecting your work, if you avoid speaking in public, if you turn down certain recording opportunities that trigger your fear, if you lose sleep before a presentation, or must resort to tranquilizers or other extreme measures, then it is vital to understand the psychological root of the problem.

The Psychology of Speech Fright

Speaking before an audience is one of the most consciousness-raising experiences a person can have.

Step into the limelight and you are flooded with awareness.

When we speak in public, reputation and career can be at stake. We are afraid of appearing unprofessional or foolish, of saying the wrong thing, of embarrassing ourselves or making a mistake.

We worry about the audience.

Will they be receptive, tune us out, or throw rotten fruit? We worry about the medium. Will the microphone work? Will the multimedia presentation crash and burn? Will we look OK on television?

Some people feel ashamed and inadequate. Others fear failure, criticism, and humiliation.

As these feelings mount, the speaker feels as if he must flee the platform or die.

Enlightening and entertaining others, helping them by sharing information that has been carefully researched and developed should be a positive, uplifting experience.

Yet why does something so good fill so many people with dread?

I found many of the answers to my questions in the work of Brazilian psychoanalysts, Dr. Norberto Keppe, founder of the International Society of Analytical Trilogy (Integral Psychoanalysis) and his associate, Dr. Claudia Pacheco.

I met Drs. Keppe and Pacheco several years ago when they were living and working in the United States and have been a student of Dr. Keppe's work ever since.

Both have been instrumental in helping me understand the psychology of communication problems, and I am deeply grateful for their profound insights and support.

It is difficult to do justice to Dr. Keppe's work in a few brief pages. He developed his methodology during more than 50 years of clinical research and has written more than 40 books.

Yet, I will do the best I can because I believe his insights provide hope and help for those who suffer from speech fright.

When Dr. Keppe investigated the inner core of the human personality, he found that human nature is profoundly different from what Freud believed. Keppe observed that our essential nature, or Being, is oriented toward life, love, truth, and beauty; not toward death and destruction as Freud proposed.

Dr. Keppe concluded that we become stressed and sick because we are not true to our inner selves. We adopt destructive attitudes that go against our essential nature, which is good, beautiful, and truthful.

Fortunately, though, we are blessed with consciousness, an inner sense of awareness that enables us to perceive these destructive attitudes so we can correct them and get ourselves back on track.

Keppe found that we distort reality by attempting to deny our fallibility.

We prefer to fantasize that it is possible to be godlike, perfect, and error free. Thus, we set all kinds of unreasonable expectations for our performance and are devastated when we are unable to meet them.

Many phobic speakers suffer from this exaggerated yet unconscious form of perfectionism, which Keppe calls theomania — the hidden desire in all human hearts to be other than we are.

According to Keppe, phobic individuals are not so much afraid of speaking as they are afraid of accepting the consciousness of their fallibility, which public speaking (and recording voice-overs) might reveal.

Another of the core concepts discovered by Dr. Keppe, which relates to speech fright, and nervousness when performing voice overs, is the phenomenon of inversion.

Keppe noted that his patients who engaged in addictive, alienating, or dangerous acts did so because they mistakenly believed guilty pleasures were beneficial in some way.

Conversely, he noted that people have an unconscious tendency to resist, and even attempt to destroy, what is clearly best for them in life. The expression "Love hurts" is an example of this.

Inversion, then, leads us to resist those activities, such as preparing a presentation or starting a new voice over business, that may be challenging, but ultimately are good for our personal and professional growth.

A good presentation is an act of love and dedication. It can take days or even weeks to prepare even the shortest talk, and all the while the speaker must struggle with procrastination.

Then they must find a way to present the material in a manner that is meaningful to the audience, using every trick at their disposal to capture and engage listener attention.

They must set their own ego aside and speak to the audience in a way they can understand.

And despite nervousness and fear, the speaker must deliver a talk or voice-over without the audience tuning them out.

Despite the hard work, the benefits of giving a successful presentation are great.

But if we unconsciously feel that contributing to others is somehow harmful to us, we will never allow ourselves to put forth the effort required to reap the rewards.

Conquering the Physical Symptoms of Speech-Fright

The physical symptoms we associate with speech fright, or performance anxiety, as scary as they may be, are actually symptoms of a temporary overabundance of stress-related hormones in the bloodstream.

These hormones — adrenaline and nor-adrenaline — affect our entire body. When they flood the bloodstream in response to stress, our breathing becomes shallow and more rapid, our heartbeat increases, our pupils dilate, and our muscles become tense.

Mike is a subscriber to my Inside Voice Over ezine (www.greatvoice.com). He wrote to me after landing a "dream job" as a TV sports commentator.

Unfortunately, he found that while he was on camera his throat would tense up and he would feel, as he put it, "a desperate need to swallow."

Sometimes this sensation would cause him to stumble verbally and lose his place while on the air.

Mike's "desperate need to swallow" is a stress-related symptom.

As Dr. Pacheco writes in *Healing Through Consciousness* (www.protonpublish-inghouse.com), when we feel fear or anger, our body secretes excess adrenaline, noradrenaline, and acetylcholine.

This directly affects the secretion of saliva (either too much or too little), affecting in turn the hydration of the mucus membranes of the mouth and throat, causing dryness and the uncomfortable symptoms Mike described.

I asked Mike what his new job meant to him. He said:

> 66 Recognition, power, success, and excitement, a chance to do what I always wanted."

He also associated the job with an important opportunity for professional advancement and personal development, a milestone in his career, the attainment of a long-cherished goal.

The fact that his "desperate need to swallow" made him fear his speech would be interrupted can be interpreted as Mike's unconscious attempt to "interrupt" his professional development and impede himself from reaching his goals.

Note Mike's inversion.

Rationally he knew the promotion was a good thing, that it would mean career advancement, recognition, and success.

But emotionally he rejected the advancement, reacting with fear and stress.

Being on TV put Mike in touch with two opposing forces of action and reaction: one moving toward career development and the other moving away from it.

Why Do So Many People Fear Success?

Have you ever wondered why so many people seem to fear success?

Consider this. When we decide to move ahead in life, to accomplish something truly worthwhile, we inevitably must face challenges and solve problems. There are new skills to master.

Take our friend Mike, for example.

In his old job on the radio, he was an expert sportscaster. But for his new job on TV, he needed to develop a whole new set of skills and face new challenges.

The more positive and worthy the endeavor, the more likely we are to come face to face with the stuff we are made of.

The more we try to grow, the more we are forced to confront our flaws, the gaps in our knowledge, our self-importance, our petty jealousies, our relationship problems, and even those problems outside of our control in society and the world around us.

These moments of truth can be a painful reality check, especially if we have harbored fantasies or grandiose ideas about ourselves.

But the more we are willing to look at how far offtrack we are, the more we will be able to keep ourselves on course.

Why Am I So Afraid of the Audience?

Many speakers say they feel nervous because they are fearful of the audience. They fear being judged, criticized, or forced to confront a barrage of hostile questions.

But while some audience members may be critical and even hostile, most people who come to hear us speak are well intentioned. They want to learn something. They want us to succeed.

Otherwise, why would they spend valuable time and even money to come hear us speak?

If you are well prepared, if you know your stuff and know your audience and if you design your presentation to meet their needs, then rationally, you should expect to be well received.

But if you still feel as if the audience is against you, you may be experiencing a common psychological phenomenon known as projection.

Here, we unconsciously project attitudes that originate within ourselves onto others because we prefer not to see those attitudes within ourselves.

For example, if we associate an audience

with hostility and criticism when there is no apparent reason for doing so and if we associate public speaking with professional growth and development, we are most likely projecting our self-critical attitudes outwardly onto others.

It means that we prefer not to see how harshly we criticize ourselves and how (because of our inversion) we are hostile to the growth and development that public speaking represents.

I have had the opportunity to observe many people in many countries while working with them on their voice and presentation skills.

And I have had the opportunity to deeply analyze my own communication problems, fears, and failures.

One core truth emerges: a critical audience is nothing compared to the ferocity with which we criticize and bash ourselves.

In speaking and in life, we set superhuman standards of perfection for ourselves and then attempt to censor any evidence that shows us we are not as we imagine ourselves to be.

I have trained entire roomfuls of people where every single person was convinced that their own voice was positively awful, even if their voice was pleasant and good.

It took me years of getting paid for doing voice-overs before I could admit that my voice was probably OK.

Just about everyone thinks their voice is too nasal, though few voices actually are.

I've heard women with deep, rich voices say they think their voice is squeaky and high.

I've seen men who speak too slowly insist they talk too fast. I've heard strong, effective speakers tell me they thought they sounded wimpy and weak.

In order to grow in any field, you need to get objective feedback. That's why even world-class athletes and performers have coaches.

Balanced, supportive feedback — providing a realistic picture of how you are perceived by others — is vital for anyone who wants to attain voice mastery and become a confident, effective voice-over artist.

Managing Adrenaline: The Essentials

As we saw previously, adrenaline causes many of the uncomfortable symptoms of speech fright.

It is the fight or flight hormone whose purpose is to help us react to danger.

But unfortunately, adrenaline can flood the bloodstream at the most inopportune times, causing your body to react as if it must run from a snarling tiger when all you have to do is give a talk to your ski club or spend a few productive hours in your home recording studio!

There are many things you can do to cope with the symptoms of speech fright.

Techniques such as physical exercises and deep breathing are useful, but they are not nearly as effective as working on the emotional root of the problem.

Dr. Pacheco says that when a person or a situation makes us nervous, it is because they remind us of something we do not want to see deep within ourselves.

The minute we feel angry, frustrated, or irritated, she suggests we stop, think, and free associate.

Free association works like this. Let's say you have to make a big presentation to Ms. Tough, a new client. You've met her before, and she makes you very nervous.

To free associate, think about Ms. Tough and notice what comes to mind.

Maybe you think she's very critical, that she dislikes you or wants to see you fail.

Now turn the ideas you have about Ms. Tough around and try to put them inside you.

When you do, you'll see that Ms. Tough is probably showing you some things about yourself that you would rather not see.

This process is called interiorization.

Ms. Tough may indeed be a very critical person. But her critical nature would not bother you much if you were willing to see the same critical attitude within yourself.

Dr. Pacheco assures us that free association and interiorization will help calm us down, not just before a presentation or voice-over recording session but at any time.

Next, get back on track by realigning yourself with your highest and best intention.

Before going in front of any audience, including the audience you picture in your mind's eye when you record your voice-over, take a moment to focus on what you have to give.

Think about how your message will help those who hear you; note how it will enrich them or improve their lives.

Get firm about your decision to give of yourself, to help and be of service in any way you can.

Step forward with the conviction that even if you stumble or make a mistake, you can easily correct it in post production.

Positive, uplifting, loving thoughts such as these have the power to completely obliterate fear.

Managing Adrenaline: The Particulars

Get Moving: Burn off excess adrenaline by getting some exercise. Take a brisk walk around the building or up and down the hall.

Push a Wall: Actors use this isometric exercise to beat stage fright.

Stand a few feet away from a wall and carefully lunge against it, one leg forward, one leg back, making sure you do not strain your knees in any way.

While in the lunge position, attempt to push the wall away from you with your hands.

Push as hard as you can, and then relax. Alternate pushing and relaxing until you feel your stress level diminish.

By the way, if you succeed in actually pushing the wall over, give me a call. I know a director who's doing a remake of Samson and Delilah who wants to hear from you.

Do Some Secret Isometrics: This is great when you can't get out of the room to exercise or push a wall.

While waiting to speak, create muscle tension by sitting up in your chair and pressing your feet firmly into the ground.

At the same time, press your arms against the sides of the chair or against your lap.

Press the small of your back against the back of the chair. Hold this position for a long count of three. Then relax to a long count of three and repeat as needed.

This exercise is great because it can be done in secret anywhere.

Not only does it diminish nerves, it also helps increase physical vitality.

Make a Joyful Noise: Another great way to burn adrenaline is to speak or sing out loud. Practice your script at full volume.

Sing in the shower or in the car on the way to the event or the recording studio.

Singing will also warm up your voice.

Cut Back on Caffeine Before a Presentation or Recording Session: Too much coffee or tea can rev you up and make the symptoms of stress even worse.

Surround Yourself with Beauty: Some soothing music, a bouquet of flowers, or a few moments spent communing with nature will help lift your spirits and inspire you.

Don't Apologize for Nervousness: Some speakers assume their nervousness must be so obvious to others that they open their talk with an apology.

But nervousness feels worse than it looks. The audience can't see your pounding heart or sweaty palms, and the voice-over director probably won't hear it in your voice, so don't call it to their attention.

If you admit to being nervous, the audience will become distracted from your message and the director might worry whether you'll make it through the recording session.

If Your Voice Trembles, Breathe Deeply: Muscle tension is constricting your diaphragm, causing you to speak on insufficient air.

Counter this effect by breathing deeply before you begin to speak.

Doing so should give your voice all the support it needs to come out clear and strong.

Practice Makes Perfect: In her book *Secrets of Successful Speakers*, Lilly Walters says that 75% of stage fright can be reduced by rehearsal and preparation, 15% by deep breathing, and the remaining 10% by mental preparation.

When practicing, read the presentation or script through several times to yourself.

Then read it several times aloud, practicing in front of a mirror.

Next, tape yourself while practicing on audio and video if possible.

Finally, practice in front of friends and family members and ask for feedback.

Prepare to Succeed: It is a good idea to gather at least seven times as much useful information as you will actually use.

It was said that Winston Churchill took

eight hours to write a 45-minute speech.

Visualize Success: Supplement the run-through of your material with positive visualization.

Athletes do this all the time, and it has been proven to enhance performance.

As soon as you are scheduled for a speaking engagement, a recording job, or a meeting with a new client, set aside a few minutes daily to imagine yourself having a successful speaking experience.

Speech fright needn't hold you back from a successful voice-over career. Neither should the lack of a recording studio.

In the next chapter, I will show you how to set up an inexpensive, easy-to-use studio at home.

SEVEN

How to Set Up an Inexpensive, Easy-to-Use Home Studio

W hen you think about a home recording studio, do you visualize one of those giant, scary-looking audio mixing boards, full of wires and dials — something that looks like the flight deck of the Starship Enterprise with James T. Kirk at the helm?

Well, erase that image from your mind right away because nothing could be further from the truth!

Today's basic home voice-over studio can be as simple as the computer you already have, a plug-in USB microphone, and a pair of headphones.

Many people record in their walk-in closet where the acoustics are excellent.

Or if you don't have an available closet, you can set up a pretty good recording space in the corner of a room lined with moving blankets or comforters.

And you don't have to be a crackerjack audio engineer, either. At The Great Voice Company, we're experts at helping beginners.

Contact us at 800-333-8108 or support@greatvoice.com to find out how we can help you.

As your business grows, you can look into upgrading your equipment and investing in a freestanding portable voice booth, but to get started, an inexpensive solution will work just fine.

The 3 Types of Home Studios

Many professional voice-over artists have several types of recording setups for different purposes.

I have equipment I can put into a carry-on bag and take on the road. It consists of my laptop (or iPad/tablet) loaded with inexpensive and easy-to-use recording software and a USB mic. Let's call this a Level One studio.

I also have a broadcast-quality Level Two studio at home that consists of an Apogee USB microphone, and a small three-sided portable recording booth lined with sound-absorptive foam that sits on my desk.

The microphone sits inside the booth and provides better sound because of the foam. There's no need to stick my head inside the portable recording booth.

I just keep my mouth pointed toward the

open end of the portable recording booth a few inches away from the mic.

Finally, I have a broadcast-quality Level Three professional studio at The Great Voice Company headquarters.

I have two audio engineers on staff and a sound isolation booth at our headquarters, and this is where we do the recording and editing work to serve our customers.

When I'm in the office, I record for my voice-over customers in this studio.

My audio engineers also coordinate recording sessions and editing projects in all languages from freelance voice talents all over the world.

But don't worry. You don't have to lease office space and hire staff like I did.

Most voice talents are one-person businesses working from home.

Now, let's take a closer look at the equipment you'll need for your home studio and some of the costs.

USB Microphones

Professional-quality USB microphones plug directly into your computer. They are a great cost-effective solution for the beginning voice talents.

New USB microphones are being introduced all the time, and the quality keeps getting better and better.

For about $200, you can have an excellent quality USB mic that emulates a much more expensive microphone.

Here are two favorite USB microphones as of the time I wrote this book:

The Apogee (about $200). The Apogee USB mic is compact, lightweight, and sounds like a much more expensive microphone. It will work with either a PC or a Mac and comes with an adapter for use with an iPad.

What I really like about this mic is that it has its own gain control. Many of the USB mics do not. The Apogee is my favorite travel mic.

The Blue Yeti (about $120). This sturdy, bullet-shaped USB mic works with a PC or a Mac and comes with its own solid metal stand to sit firmly on your desk. It has a gain control, and many people love the way it sounds.

The store where you buy your USB microphone can let you know about the latest models available when you're ready to buy.

You might find an even better mic than the ones I have listed here.

Upgrading Your Microphone

Prices for upgraded mics start around $300 and climb to thousands of dollars.

These upgraded mics do not plug directly into your computer and will require an interface or microphone pre-amp.

The microphone plugs into the pre-amp and the pre-amp plugs into your computer's USB port. You can get a good-quality USB pre-amp for as little as $100.

The better-quality microphones are more sensitive, so they will also require more sound-proofing.

For a beginner, a good-quality USB microphone is fine. I recommend that you upgrade later as you begin to get more work.

Headphones

Another piece of essential gear you'll need is studio-quality headphones. They do the job much more effectively than computer speakers, even the more expensive ones.

I recommend the Sennheiser HD 280 Pro or the Sony MDR 7506. Either one is of excellent quality and costs about $99. They close over the ear to shut out background noise so you can hear everything you've recorded.

Cheap headphones or earbuds just won't do, although I sometimes use high-quality Bose ear buds (about $200) in my portable recording setup when I travel.

Here's a headphone tip: Make sure you do not use noise-canceling headphones, such as the ones people wear on airplanes.

In voice-over you want to hear the noise

so you can edit it out of the finished product.

Audio-Recording Software

Audio-recording software is a tool for editing your sound files. You'll cut and paste these files and move them around just as you would move words around in your favorite word-processing software.

More expensive software will not make your voice sound better.

In fact, it might even confuse you with advanced features you do not need. For most people, a free audio-recording software called Audacity is fine.

We use Sony Sound Forge Audio Studio on the PCs at The Great Voice Company, and I use Twisted Wave on my MAC. I like both a lot.

If you have a MAC, I do not recommend the free GarageBand software that came with it. It is designed for musicians, and it is difficult to use for voice-over work, adding effects you don't need, like reverb.

I suggest downloading some free trials of various recording software until you find one you like.

Finding the Best Place in Your Home to Record

Many people use a walk-in closet, and it's even better if you don't remove the clothes.

Fabric helps dampen the sound.

Of course, you may have to move a few things around to get set up.

If your computer is noisy, consider leaving it outside the closet and getting a long mic cord or remote control.

If you're buying a new computer look for one with a solid state hard drive. They have no moving parts, and are nearly silent.

You'll need a stand for your microphone and a music stand with an LED light to hold your copy.

I like to load my scripts onto an iPad, tablet or even my smartphone if the script is short.

These solutions make the text easy to see in a dimly lit area, and there is no noise when I turn the page. Plus, I don't have to worry about a printer or paper.

If you don't have an available closet, the best place to record is in the quietest room in the house facing a corner away from windows.

Hang a comforter or a moving blanket in the corner behind your mic and talk into the mic facing the corner.

Basements are also good places to record if you locate yourself away from noisy laundry rooms and heating and air conditioning units.

Make sure you put a sign on the door reminding your house mates to be quiet, turn off your cell phone, and remove any panting dogs or meddlesome cats from the room.

What if You Book a Job and Your Home Studio Isn't Ready Yet?

Easy! Simply book time in an outside studio and pass along the cost to your customer.

Studios sell the time by the hour and prices vary, so ask around. Depending on where you live, you can probably rent time in a good, professional-quality studio for a simple voice-over session for less than $100 an hour.

You'll include these costs in the rates you charge your client.

There's an entire chapter on how much to charge for your work later in the book.

But for now, let's focus on 14 real ways to make real money with your voice in Chapter 8.

PART II

EIGHT

The Amazing Power of the Voice-Over Niche

T here is a huge secret in voice-overs that only the top earners figure out and use to their advantage. Most others remain ignorant, but some see it and never quite figure out how to make this secret work for them.

The big secret is this: There are riches in voice-over niches.

A niche market is a small market segment, a narrow group of customers with a specific set of needs.

I've identified 14 different voice-over niches where you can make really good money with your voice, and we'll explore them in this chapter.

Some people stubbornly insist on trying to be all things to all people, thinking that the more variety they can offer potential customers, the greater their chances of success.

They put a little bit of everything on

their demos, trying to do as many different types of voices as they can.

Having a flexible voice with a big range is a nice talent to have, but if you don't have a lot of different voices, you can still have a very successful career.

It's important not to push the envelope and try to be someone you're not.

I was once guilty of this mistake.

On an early voice-over demo of mine, I included a really bad witch voice thinking that maybe people would like to hear that I was able to do cartoon and character voices in addition to my warm, yet authoritative signature sound.

My attempt to show variety backfired when a talent agent told me point-blank how bad my witch voice sounded and that I should never attempt to do a voice like that again.

How embarrassing!

Since then, I've learned to stick to what I do best, working in niches that appreciate my signature sound.

The fact is, as you progress in your voice-over career, you'll be paid the most for your most authentic and believable voice, not for being a poor imitation of somebody else.

Why Choosing a Voice-Over Niche Market is the Fastest and Best Way to Accelerate Your Success

Specialists are More Highly Paid: Your family physician might be fine for run-of-the-mill health problems.

But heaven forbid you or someone you love needs help for a more serious illness. I doubt you'd walk into the urgent care clinic in the local strip mall looking for help. You'd want to see a specialist, an expert on your condition.

The bill, when it comes, will be hefty and you can hope insurance will cover it.

But it's what you'd expect from a specialist, especially someone who really understands your particular situation.

Building your voice-over career as a specialist in a niche market is a proven way to separate yourself from the pack and command premium prices for your work.

Voice Buyers Think in Terms of Types: Make it easy for them. Some people are uncomfortable being typecast.

They want to be known for their uniqueness as an individual.

Scripts, however, are written to appeal to very specific market segments and are written with specific voice types in mind.

Agents and casting directors classify talent according to types.

It makes their job easier, and they use the language of types when referring to the voices in their talent pool.

Certain voice types are appropriate for certain niche markets, and in a moment I'll show you how to match your voice type to a niche market where you'll have the best advantage.

A Confused Person Does _Not_ Buy: Ever walk out of a store because you are too confused to make a decision on what to buy?

I know I have.

In fact, after a long day's work, I even dread going to the supermarket because the thought of all that variety taxes my brain.

Which spaghetti sauce tastes best?

Sometimes it's better to just get take out so I don't have to deal with it.

Positioning yourself as an expert in a voice-over niche removes a layer of complexity from the voice buyer's life and makes it a relief and a pleasure to hire you.

A Niche Market is Easier to Find: You might not realize how many voice-over jobs are cast and recorded every day in each of the 14 niche markets — tens of thousands!

Trying to market your services to all those buyers is like trying to sell to everyone in the phone book, an impossible task.

Choose a niche, however, and your task becomes a whole lot easier.

Every niche has associations, listings, publications, social media groups, conferences, and the like.

When you choose a niche, the target becomes clear and your business-building efforts become laser focused.

Focus Gives You Power: Once you discover your target niche market, you can narrow your focus with laser-like precision.

Like an elite athlete, you'll have one goal — to win the race.

Here's a tip: Create a Dream 100 list of the top prospects in your niche and mount focused campaigns to reach them.

Research them on LinkedIn and set Google alerts so you can track them online to refine your sales and marketing efforts.

What a Voice-Over Niche Is Not

Before I get into specifics about the 14 niche voice-over markets, I'd like to clarify what a niche is not since people sometimes get confused.

- A niche is not a cute slogan like the "voice chick," "the voice of choice," or "voices of experience."
- A niche is not your logo or your brand.
- A niche is not your voice type, such as smooth and reassuring, warm yet

authoritative, deep and resonant, etc.
- A niche is not your swag (free giveaways), such as tote bags, T-shirts, and mouse pads.

So, if a niche isn't any of these things, what is it? A niche is nothing more than a group of prospective customers.

The WHO Is More Important Than the What

One of the biggest mistakes I see voice-over beginners make, or newcomers in any business for that matter, is that they focus on the product (the what) before they carefully analyze who will use the product.

Have you ever heard the saying "Build it and they will come"?

It's from the movie Field of Dreams.

Well, that saying might have worked in Hollywood, but in real life, it doesn't work at all and is probably responsible for more business failures than anything else.

People who put their energy into building a product or presenting a service before they carefully analyze who that product or service will be for are likely doomed to failure.

It's the same in voice-over.

I always help my students determine their ideal group of customers first, based on their natural strengths and abilities and the professional skills they bring to the table.

Then, we match these skills with the market(s) that will appreciate and value them the most.

This is your low-hanging fruit, where you will have the greatest chances of success.

To help you identify the strengths you bring to the table, I've developed the following quiz. Your answers will help you match your strengths to the niche where they will be most appreciated and valued.

My Easy Niche-Finder Quiz

Are you a fluid reader, comfortable reading long passages of text without stumbling a lot?

❏ Yes   ❏ No

Do you prefer shorter scripts?

❏ Yes   ❏ No

Are you comfortable reading medical or technical terms (long, difficult-to-pronounce words)?

❏ Yes   ❏ No

Are you a medical professional?

❏ Yes   ❏ No

Would you enjoy doing characters/cartoons?

❏ Yes   ❏ No

Have you ever taught or trained people?

❏ Yes ❏ No

Would you enjoy reading instructional scripts?

❏ Yes ❏ No

Are you naturally enthusiastic with a lot of energy in your voice?

❏ Yes ❏ No

Can you speak quickly yet clearly?

❏ Yes ❏ No

Do you speak a language other than English fluently like a native?

❏ Yes ❏ No

Do you listen to audio books and would you enjoy being an audio book narrator?

❏ Yes ❏ No

Would you enjoy learning about home recording and some easy-to-master recording skills?

❏ Yes ❏ No

Are you timid about computers and a little intimidated by new technology?

❏ Yes ❏ No

Do you enjoy playing around with audio gear and learning new computer programs?

❏ Yes   ❏ No

Do you have a radio or television background?

❏ Yes   ❏ No

Have you ever done any acting on stage or film (even as an amateur or in school)?

❏ Yes   ❏ No

Do you have specialized technical skills/training?

❏ Yes   ❏ No

Do you have a professional background in law, financial services, or engineering?

❏ Yes   ❏ No

Do you have security clearance?

❏ Yes   ❏ No

As you go through the opportunities in the 14 Voice-Over Niches in the next chapter, note which of your strengths apply.

NINE

Money-Making Opportunities in the 14 Voice-Over Niche Markets and How to Choose the Voice-Over Niche That's Right for You

I n this chapter I'll help you pick a niche market where your life experience and skills give you an edge, a niche that's right for your signature sound and voice type.

If you're feeling a little stressed about which voice-over niche is right for you, I'd like to put your mind at ease.

You're not making a permanent decision here.

I'm merely trying to help you find the low-hanging fruit and give you a starting point with the best competitive advantage and market segments where you have the best likelihood of success.

And here's some good news.

If the niche you choose to start with doesn't work out, there are always 13 more niches to choose from — you can't go wrong!

Niche #1:
Commercials: Radio, TV, and Internet

When people think of voice-overs, they typically think commercials.

After all, commercials are everywhere, and who wouldn't like to be the voice on a Super Bowl commercial, right?

But the truth is, even if you never become the voice of a national campaign, there's still plenty of opportunity.

It's hard to know exactly how many commercials are cast every day, but we can make an educated guess.

In the United States, there are more than 11,000 commercial radio stations and more than 300 broadcast and cable television networks.

If you figure each one of these outlets runs about 20 minutes of advertising every hour, that's over 5.4 million minutes of broadcast advertising nationwide per day!

Even if we cut that number in half, that's still a heck of a lot of commercials (not even including commercials on the internet), and it's impossible for celebrities to do all that work.

If you've ever gone to YouTube to watch a video, you'll see that you usually have to sit through a commercial before the video will play.

Even though the actors are on camera,

there's almost always an off-camera voice actor in the spot.

That's why we suggest that our students make a commercial demo as part of their portfolio.

It's a competitive market to be sure, but there's no lack of opportunity.

Commercial voice-overs are cast by agents, casting directors, advertising agencies, and sometimes, the clients themselves.

There are opportunities for all voice types and all vocal age ranges.

Pay careful attention the next time you watch TV or listen to the radio. You are sure to hear a voice that is similar to yours.

It used to be that commercials were voiced by middle-aged white men who sounded like Richard Burton or god.

You scarcely heard a woman on the air, let alone a voice that was recognizable as belonging to a person of color.

These days, all that has changed.

The range of voice types being used in commercials is becoming more and more diverse.

Do you speak Spanish like a native?

If so, you may have a future in Spanish-language commercials.

People who are fluent in both English and Spanish often enjoy successful voice-over careers in both languages.

Niche in a Nutshell: Commercials

- ❏ Scripts: short

- ❏ Most work comes from auditions

- ❏ Agents and casting services send you auditions

- ❏ Audition from your home studio

- ❏ You need a good-quality home studio or be willing to record in a professional studio nearby

- ❏ A director might want to direct you when you record

- ❏ Open to all voice types

- ❏ Pay (varies widely): $50 for a local radio commercial to $1,000+ for a national TV voice-over

Niche #2:
Non-Broadcast Corporate Voice-Overs

Corporate voice-over work is the bread and butter for most voice actors.

Billions of dollars are spent on corporate production every year. I call this a "hidden niche" because the work is not broadcast on television or radio, but is used internally and within an industry. Nevertheless, there's a lot of work in this area with a big potential for repeat business.

Corporate voice-overs include web videos, promotional pieces, sales pieces for trade shows, employee training, and the like.

Producers of corporate audio typically cast from demos. Auditions are rare. The voice buyer might call the talent directly or work through an agent. Scripts can be quite short to many hundreds of pages long. The average script is about 5-10 pages long.

There are no residuals, but once you've proven yourself to be professional and easy to work with, there is repeat business.

Niche in a Nutshell: Corporate Voice-Overs

- ❏ Scripts: all lengths
- ❏ Auditions are rare
- ❏ Work can come through agents or production companies
- ❏ No residuals but repeat business if you do a good job
- ❏ Open to all voice types except children
- ❏ Pay: by the hour, by the page, or by the word (Example: $250+ $0.40-$0.50/word)

Niche #3:
Audio Books

According to a recent survey published by the Audio Publishers Association, audio books are a $2 billion+ a year industry that keeps on growing.

U.S. audio book sales in 2020 totaled about $2 billion, up 16% from the previous year, continuing an eight-year trend of double-digit growth.

Audio book publishers reported there were 60,303 new titles produced in 2019 alone!

People love the convenience of listening to audio books, especially in the car.

They find it relaxing and a good way to multitask.

But while the audio book niche is growing exponentially, becoming an audio book narrator is not for everyone.

It is by far the most time-intensive genre of voice acting work, requiring stamina, solid voice acting skills, a healthy vocal instrument, and some degree of audio engineering skills.

To give you an idea of the time commitment involved, it takes approximately five hours to record and edit a single hour of finished audio.

The finished listening time of the average book is about eight hours (some are 12 hours or more), so that means a good 24 to 45 hours must be spent, on average, recording and editing a book.

While you can start as an audio book narrator with a fairly small investment, recording in a closet on an inexpensive microphone and editing on free recording software, the most successful narrators invest thousands of dollars in upgraded studio equipment.

Audio book narrators are paid by the finished hour with an average rate of $250 to \$400 per finished hour. Narrators can also enter into a royalty share agreement with the publisher or author on the Audiobook Creation Exchange site at **www.acx.com.**

Niche in a Nutshell: Audio Books

❑ Scripts: hundreds of pages

❑ Work is booked through publishers, *www.acx.com,* and internet casting sites

❑ Acting or narration experience a plus

❑ Many genres: business, fiction, science fiction, children's, etc.

❑ Audio engineering skills required

❑ Pay: \$250-\$400/per finished hour or as royalty share with publisher or author

Niche #4:
Book Trailers

Book trailers are a new niche, closely tied to the growth of the audio book industry.

To promote a book, publishers and authors create video promotions; the average book trailer is several minutes long.

While some book trailers are rudimentary and poorly produced, cinematic book trailers fall someplace between a movie trailer and a short film.

They're a lot like music videos in terms of form.

Cinematic book trailers are created to give the viewer a taste of the tone, pacing, and details of the book to create an interest in the book and its author.

Most book trailers feature voice-over, often from emerging talent. Rates for this new niche have not been well established and are negotiated between the actor and the producer.

Niche in a Nutshell: Book Trailers

❑ Scripts: short

❑ Work is cast by book trailer production house

❑ Acting experience a plus

❑ Minimal audio engineering skills required; you'll record in a studio or from home, directed by the producer

❑ Pay: negotiable

Niche #5:
Medical Narrations

Do you have a medical or pharmaceutical background?

Are you comfortable with the terminology, and can you properly pronounce those big, technical words?

More important, can you tell the story behind the words so you really connect with patients and health care professionals and sound as if you know what you are talking about?

Medical narrators work for medical marketing and media companies.

These companies produce medical education for patients and practitioners alike.

They produce online medical courses, multimedia medical presentations, medical narrations, medical animations, instructional programs and promotions for medical conferences, pharmaceutical product launches, and special interactive phone systems for drug trials.

This is a large and growing market with opportunity for individuals with the right technical background and the specialized skills to handle the unique requirements of the job.

Niche in a Nutshell: Medical Narrations

- ❏ Scripts: length varies but special pronunciation skills needed

- ❏ Work is booked through medical marketing and media companies, medical service organizations, and ad agencies that work in the medical field

- ❏ Medical or technical background a plus

- ❏ Pay: by the hour, the page, or the word

- ❏ Rates vary but range from $400 for a 30-minute script to over $900 for 5,000 words; due to the specialized nature of this niche, an experienced narrator can charge more than a typical corporate narrator

Niche #6:
TV Promos

You probably don't realize how many TV promos are recorded and air every day.

There are more than 300 cable and broadcast television networks, with thousands of shows running around the clock.

The next time you watch your favorite show, notice the professional voice that opens and closes the shows and speaks before and after the commercials.

These voices also promote the shows in promotional announcements during commercial breaks throughout the broadcast day.

Promo voice talents have the ability to inject focused energy into their reads. The scripts are quite short, but a good sense of timing is critical.

In recent years, there's been a shift away from an announcer sound to a more casual, conversational style. Therefore, this niche is opening up to a wider variety of voice types.

Once you land an opportunity as a promo announcer and become the voice associated with the show, there's lots of repeat business and frequent recording sessions.

Promo announcers are paid for the main announcement plus any "tags" they record — for example: "starts Tuesday," "starts tomorrow," "starts today."

A high-quality home studio is needed. You'll work closely with program producers and promo directors to help convey the vision and mood for the show.

Niche in a Nutshell: TV Promos

- ❏ Scripts: short; good sense of timing required

- ❏ High-quality home studio needed

- ❏ Work is booked through show producers and promo directors

- ❏ Pay: $240-$350 per session plus $93 per tag

Niche #7:
Local Cable TV

Local cable TV networks sell advertising to local businesses.

You've seen these ads, I'm sure — everything from the local home improvement company to the pet store on Main Street.

These commercials need to be profession- ally voiced, either at the television station or from the voice talent's home studio.

Because these stations are often small, the program director or sales manager hires the voice talent.

They tend to be easy to contact and appreciative of your offer to help.

Although the pay is modest compared to network promos, there can be a lot of repeat business and working at the local level can be an ideal way to start your career.

> **Niche in a Nutshell:** Local Cable TV
> - ❑ Scripts: short; good sense of timing required
> - ❑ Record at the TV station or in your home studio
> - ❑ Work is booked through program director or sales manager
> - ❑ Pay: $50-$175 per spot

Niche #8:
Interactive Voice Response (IVR), Speech Recognition, Telematics (talking vehicles), Telephone Voice Prompts

As the telephone voice of AT&T and Citibank, I have a lot of experience in this niche.

In fact, I've built a whole career around it and must have recorded millions of prompts.

Today, voices are embedded in many kinds of devices beyond telephones.

Almost everything talks, and a voice actor recorded each voice.

This niche tends to favor female voices, although men are also used.

You need good diction, clear speech, a healthy vocal instrument, and a lot of stamina, as recording sessions can require you to read hundreds of short voice prompts in one sitting.

You'll record everything from GPS systems to banking information to security alerts to information for drug trials.

A great thing about this niche is the repeat business.

Once your voice becomes embedded in a system, your customers will use you again and again, as updates are frequent.

You'll need a good-quality home studio and ready availability for quick turnaround, generally within 24 to 48 hours.

Your customers will be speech technology companies and specialized production companies (like mine).

Niche in a Nutshell:
Interactive Voice Response

❑ Scripts: short individual phrases within scripts that can be many pages long

❑ Record from your home studio

❑ Work is booked through technology companies and production

❑ Pay: minimum of $100 for a handful of prompts to $10,000 or more for a large technology application where many thousands of prompts are recorded

Niche #9:
Animation

If you are attracted to this niche, you know who you are. You love cartoons and animated movies and probably have your own stable of unique and original character voices.

In addition to animation for kids, there is a strong adult-oriented animation market with voices needed for action-adventure productions that are definitely R-rated!

Animation voice specialists work not just in cartoons, but also in commercials and other animated presentations.

Los Angeles is the mecca for animation, with work also being done in Orlando, Florida, for the attractions industry and in Toronto, Canada, for an emerging animation market-place.

Voice talents who live outside these markets are able to do some of this work from home.

Work is cast through talent agents, casting directors, animation houses, and producers. While work can be done from a home studio, actors are often required to work in a professional studio where they will be directed as part of an ensemble cast.

Actors are often required to voice several characters in each production and are paid to voice a minimum of three voices in each cartoon.

Niche in a Nutshell: Animation, Cartoons

- ❑ Scripts: length varies; specialized voice acting skills required

- ❑ Record in a professional studio or at home

- ❑ Work is booked through agents, casting directors, and production companies

- ❑ Pay: $600-$900 for up to three voices in a program, depending on program length; residuals paid for union work depending on the production company agreement, and usage fees can be negotiated for non-union work

Niche #10:
Video Games/Interactive

The video game industry is experiencing explosive growth. Fifty-eight percent of Americans play video games.

The average U.S. household owns at least one video game console, PC, or smartphone on which video games are played.

In 2020, consumers spent a record $56.9 billion on video games. All types of voices are used for video games, but high energy and strong acting ability is required.

Listen to a few video games and you'll know what I mean. While action adventure is a popular genre, there are also video games based on popular TV shows, as well as video games for little kids.

Work is cast through talent agents, casting directors, and video game production companies.

Niche in a Nutshell:
Video Games/Interactive

❏ Scripts: length varies; specialized voice acting skills required

❏ Record in a professional studio or at home

❏ Work is auditioned for and booked through agents, casting directors, and video game production companies

❏ Pay: varies by production and number of voices

❏ A typical production requires up to three voices during a four-hour session; pay is about $780 (more for additional voices)

Niche #11:
E-Learning

More and more students and employees are using e-learning to earn their degrees, build their knowledge base, and develop new skills.

An increasing number of online courses are being offered to meet the ever-growing demand.

By 2026, the global e-learning market is expected to grow to $374.3 billion.

E-learning is a valuable resource for

corporations, saving businesses at least 50% over traditional instructor-based training.

Over 40% of Fortune 500 companies now use some form of technology to instruct employees.

Successful e-learning narrators typically work from home, are comfortable with longer scripts, and have voices that are warm, pleasant, and easy to listen to.

They know how to teach with their voice and lead learners through a wide range of materials, from simple to complex and technical.

Niche in a Nutshell: E-Learning

❑ Scripts: lengthy, but range from under an hour to many hours of instruction; some jobs are extensive, taking weeks or even months to record

❑ Recording is typically done in a home studio

❑ Work is done for instructional designers and e-learning companies

❑ Some clients are offshore, many in India

❑ Pay: average rate is $25 per finished minute with a 10-minute ($250) minimum; $1,500 per finished hour (Note: one finished hour of audio typically takes between three to five hours to record and edit)

Niche #12:
Foreign Languages (non-U.S. English)

Can you speak a language other than English fluently like a native? If so, you may have a valuable voice-over skill.

The biggest non-English voice-over niche is Spanish.

According to the 2020 U.S. Census, the nation's Hispanic population grew to more than 60 million or 18.5% of the U.S. population.

There are hundreds of Spanish-language radio and TV stations and many thousands of Spanish-language commercials recorded each year.

Univision, the largest Spanish-language network by far, reaches audience sizes that compete with the three major English-language broadcast networks (ABC, CBS, and NBC).

It recently launched a 24-hour Spanish-language news station.

There are also ample opportunities for Spanish-speaking voice actors in non-broadcast productions.

At The Great Voice Company, most of the voice talents we hire for phone systems and other interactive voice applications are native speakers of other languages.

We record in the major European and Asian languages as well as in some of the less widely spoken languages, such as Haitian Creole.

Speakers of other languages can also market their voice to translation, medical narration, and e-learning companies.

In languages other than Spanish, the speaker can often command a higher price because there is less competition for the work.

Niche in a Nutshell: Foreign Languages

❑ Scripts: all lengths

❑ Broadcast and non-broadcast recording

❑ Recording is done in a home studio or on site

❑ Pay: professional voice talents who speak languages other than English or Spanish can command rates that are 25%-100% higher than English, although there is less demand for their work

---

Niche #13:
Event Announcers

The major award ceremonies, such as the Academy Awards, Emmys, and Grammys, feature the voices of live announcers.

These men and women sit in a backstage booth during the ceremony and introduce the various show segments.

It's a well-paid, high-profile gig open to only a handful of experienced well-connected talents.

But did you know there are many other lesser known awards ceremonies?

Some of these are broadcast and some are not. Big corporations often hold their own awards ceremonies, typically in a hotel ballroom, to honor VIPs, clients, and top salespeople.

These event announcements are not live, but prerecorded.

For many years, I voiced the annual sales meetings for the Spencer Gifts chain of stores.

Niche in a Nutshell: Event Announcers

❏ Scripts: short segments

❏ An enthusiastic, high-energy delivery and excellent sense of timing is needed

❏ Recording is done in a home studio or live at the event

❏ Pay: varies depending on the nature of the event

Niche #14:
Political Ads

This is a highly specialized niche that coordinates with the election cycle.

Voice actors are hired to appeal to a specific electorate, and sometimes a regional accent or dialect is preferred, depending on the political race.

Clients are political advertising and marketing agencies.

Campaigns and outside groups spend billions of dollars on advertising, with as many as 73,000 spots running in battleground states. The work is seasonal and things can get really busy between Labor Day and Election Day.

In late October it's not uncommon for a political ad voice actor to do as many as 25 spots a day.

There are four styles of political voice-over: compassionate, patriotic, disenchanted, and attack — and actors must be able to do them all.

Niche in a Nutshell: Political Ads

❑ Scripts: 30-60 seconds

❑ Broadcast-quality home studio, ability to take direction, ultra fast turnaround required

❑ The director must be able to patch in to direct the talent

❑ Pay: $400-$1,000 per spot; top political voice actors can make over $100,000 during the political season

TEN

Weird and Unusual Ways to Make Money With Your Voice

Talking Toys: When I was a kid, I had a giant life-sized doll that talked when you pulled a string.

Her name was Chatty Cathy, and a voice actor recorded her voice. She sat in a chair and looked so real she scared the living daylights out of my mother.

These days, we've come a long way from pull-string toys.

There are thousands of talking toys on the market with embedded audio chips — from Despicable Me action figures to Dora the Explorer to Buzz Lightyear to Ben the Bear. Someone needs to record all those voices — it could be you!

Talking Devices: There are many devices that talk to you. I have a portable wireless speaker with a woman's voice that tells me when the device is paired with my computer or when the battery is running low.

I once forgot to turn it off and left it in a suitcase after a trip. A strange, muffled voice woke me up in the middle of the night.

Alarmed and frantic, I searched the house until I finally figured out it was my speaker! Frankly, I felt like tossing it out the window.

I'm the voice in a device that tells you where you left your keys or your glasses.

If you hear a voice while searching for your glasses in the middle of the night, don't be alarmed and please don't throw the gadget out the window. It's only me.

Museum Guide: Whenever I visit a museum, I always get the audio tour.

A voice walks me through the exhibit and gives fascinating details about the art. It really enhances the experience.

Do a Google search and you'll see about 125 million entries for museum audio tours.

Why not promote your voice to some of these companies?

Historical Sites: At Colonial Williamsburg, there are talking tree stumps at the site of the Jamestown Massacre.

Move from stump to stump and a voice gives you the historical details.

At the top of the Willis Tower in Chicago, pick up a phone and a woman tells you all about the Great Chicago Fire.

These interactive exhibits are common at historical sites all across the nation.

Poke around online and you're sure to find the companies that produce this audio.

Transportation Voice-Over: My friend Bernie Wagenblast is the voice of the New York City Subway and the monorail at Newark Airport.

There are recorded voices at airports and amusement parks everywhere. That could be you telling people to mind the closing door!

Christmas Decorations: Here's a weird one. One of our program grads, Pamela Almand, has an eccentric neighbor who does elaborate Christmas decorations — the kind you can see from an airplane.

As you drive by the decorations, you tune your car radio to the neighbor's dedicated radio station to hear Christmas music and Pam's voice wishing you holiday greetings.

She made good money for it, too.

Keep your eyes open and you might find a similar unusual voice-over opportunity near you.

Real Estate Information: Like the guy with the elaborate Christmas decorations, some real estate companies install transmitters outside homes for sale.

As you drive by, you can tune your radio and get information about the home recorded by a voice actor.

There are also real estate channels on the local cable network. Watch those shows and the production company should be listed in the credits at the end.

Give them a call and see if you can be their next voice!

Attention, Shoppers! Point of Purchase Video and Radio: Also known as POP Radio, you hear these in-store radio networks in the supermarket and chain drugstores.

Between the music, voices give recipes, share tips, and tell you about special deals.

Point of purchase videos are often found in department stores at the makeup counter and at big box retailers like Bed Bath & Beyond.

While shopping at Bed Bath & Beyond for a kitchen gadget, I heard a familiar voice.

It was my own, narrating a video for OXO! I gave the saleslady my autograph — on the credit card slip.

Do a search for point of purchase in store networks and you'll find the production companies that produce these programs and hire the voices.

ELEVEN

Putting Your Plan Into Action

Before You Start:
Seven Steps to Setting Yourself Up for Voice-Over Success

When you implement the easy strategies I outline in this book, you'll soon find that voice-over can become the ideal money hobby or work from home opportunity you've been searching for.

The sampling of success stories below illustrates the extensive possibilities you have in voice-over:

- Fee to voice a 20-page non-broadcast corporate narration piece: $700
- An extra $75 to voice a radio commercial in a small market
- $375 to narrate a three-page training video
- Fee to narrate an audio book — 8 finished hours: $4,000

- 200 telephone voice prompts: $225
- One-hour e-learning narration (finished audio): $1,200
- Huge e-learning project that took one year to record from home: $94,000
- Four-page medical narration: $750
- Video game residual check paid to union voice talent: $100,000
- Narrate an 80-page business e-book for a financial advisor: $3,400
- Large text to speech application for IBM: $10,000

These results come from people in a range of professions: teacher, retired airline pilot, corporate trainer, manager, retired architect, stay-at-home mom, IT professional, long-haul truck driver, nurse, and more.

Each has a unique goal for his or her voice-over business. Yet, in spite of these differences, all took the same three steps to achieve their success:

- **They defined a strategy for their career.**

- **They got professional training in performance, marketing, and basic home recording skills and made a professionally produced demo.**

- **They implemented their marketing plan.**

It seems so simple, yet many people miss one or more of these three steps when it comes to getting started in voice-over.

However, it's no different than developing a strategy and a marketing plan for any business.

A solid business strategy for your voice-over career is the secret to making real money with your voice.

So, where do you begin? I suggest starting with the steps below.

You'll note that each of these steps contains at least one question. The answer to these questions will help you develop a plan and strategies that will work best for you.

Here are the seven steps to Voice-Over Success:

1. Have a professional talent advisor assess your voice and review your goals.

This is the most important step to take before getting started.

Our talent advisor will listen to you read a few scripts and complete a comprehensive assessment in these key areas: diction, reading ability, voice quality, and vocal energy level.

Our advisor will also review your goals and make a recommendation about the niche markets where you'll stand the greatest chance for success.

To book a consultation contact The Great Voice Company at support@greatvoice.com.

2. *Review the opportunities in the 14 niche voice-over markets and take my easy niche-finder quiz.* Which niches appeal to you? In which of the niche markets are you able to make the most of your professional skills and life experience?

3. *Review the items you'll need for your basic Level One home studio and determine the best place in your home to record.* I gave you an overview of your home studio in Chapter 6.

4. Develop your list of friends and promoters who can help you. It's likely you already know one or more people who know someone who hires voice talent.

This will be the first place you go when you're ready to launch your new voice-over business.

5. *Learn how to have a voice-over demo that gets you noticed and gets you work.* Before you get hired, all prospective customers will want to hear a professionally produced sample of your work.

This voice-over demo is your key marketing piece, but it must be properly and strategically produced.

Voice-Over demos are short — typically no longer than 90 seconds. The demo is a compilation of several pieces of copy to showcase your voice and performance skills.

Many voice-over artists have several demos, one for each niche market, featuring scripts from that niche.

Our coaches work with you to select the scripts and help you prepare for your recording session. They will direct you in your headphones as you record.

It typically takes an hour to record your demo voice tracks. Then we select the music and edit and produce the voice tracks, delivering the finished demo to you in about two weeks.

But before you walk into a studio to record your demo, you must determine a strategy to reach your target niche market, and you must be properly trained. Without this preparation, you'll be wasting your time and your money.

At The Great Voice Company, we've devised a carefully curated and customized Voice-Over Training Institute program that enables most people to launch their voice-over career in about six months.

This comprehensive program consists of a series of private video or telephone coaching sessions with one of our coaches, a custom, professionally produced demo, monthly group coaching calls, support for mindset issues, and training in how to build and implement a customized marketing program to build your career.

Contact us at support@greatvoice.com for details.

6. Set up a system that drives business to you. Your demo alone will never amount to much.

But place it within a marketing system and you'll have the power to launch a successful voice-over career in record time.

Your voice-over marketing system can include some or all of the following:

- Social media networking on LinkedIn and Facebook
- An optimized website
- Networking at local business and industry functions
- Phone and email queries
- Distributing your demo to people of influence: friends and industry professionals
- Pay-to-play casting sites
- Talent agents
- Postcards and other creative mail pieces
- Lead generation on Fiverr, Elance, and other sites

- Meeting prospective voice buyers at professional conferences

Don't be intimidated by this list or try to do everything all at once. Just choose one or two marketing strategies that appeal to you.

As they prove fruitful, you can add other strategies as you go along.

7. Get started! The next step is in your hands. I've given you advice, outlined the steps you need to take, and made specific recommendations about how to get started.

Remember, success in voice-over isn't just about your voice. It's about using your voice as a valued resource to serve your clients and customers.

Follow my road map, be of service to your clients, and you'll reap the rewards!

About Susan Berkley

As the signature telephone voice of Citibank and founder and president of The Great Voice Company at **www.greatvoice.com**, Susan Berkley is one of the most listened-to voices in America.

A former radio personality and cast member of *The Howard Stern Show*, Susan left radio to pursue her entrepreneurial dream of having a successful voice-over business.

She also devoted herself to the study of sales and marketing, systemizing a proprietary Mic to Money™ method that she teaches in her training programs.

Other voice talents call Susan "the most respected voice-over teacher alive" and the list of well-known voice talents who freely reference Susan and The Great Voice Company as their primary mentor for voice-over training is just staggering.

Her popular virtual training and coaching programs are hailed as the gold standard for hands-on voice-over learning.

Because she comes from a family of entrepreneurs (her grandfather was the co-creator of Archie Comics), Susan has a deep respect and love for great direct-response marketing that is both ethical and fun.

She long ago realized that great voice-over careers are born not by learning to audition and perform just a little bit better than everyone else, but by applying the simple secrets of proven sales and marketing techniques.

If you truly have a desire to do voice-over work and the urge to share the gift of your voice with others... then it's your job to understand how to get your message across in a way that hits home.

From developing your performance skills behind the mic to learning to record pristine, quality audio from home and then getting to work, Susan Berkley's SIMPLE Monetize Your Voice System™ takes you step-by-step through the process of starting and sustaining a great voice-over career.

Best of all, it's easy, fun... and completely removes the "sticking points" that confuse so many emerging voice talents.

If you've ever wondered how great voice-over careers are born, Susan and the team at The Great Voice Company will show you the way.

For more information on how to start your voice-over career, visit **www.greatvoice. com** or contact The Great Voice Company at support@greatvoice.com.

To help you get maximum value from this book, claim this collection of...

Free Voice-Over Resources
($97 value)
Waiting for you at:

www.GreatVoice.com/Gifts

- ✔ **FREE Audio Book:** *Voice-Over Secrets Exposed* read by Susan Berkley

- ✔ **FREE 6-Figure Voice-Over Success Roadmap:** video + workbook

- ✔ **FREE How to Get Started in Voice-Over:** 3-minute crash course

For the additional resources mentioned in this book, please visit:

www.GreatVoice.com/Gifts